The
PHOTOGUIDE
to
Flash

THE ⓟ PHOTOGUIDES

THE PHOTOGUIDE TO THE 35 mm SINGLE LENS REFLEX
THE PHOTOGUIDE TO HOME PROCESSING
THE PHOTOGUIDE TO ENLARGING
THE PHOTOGUIDE TO PORTRAITS
THE PHOTOGUIDE TO FLASH
THE PHOTOGUIDE TO EFFECTS AND TRICKS

The PHOTOGUIDE to Flash

Günter Spitzing

AMPHOTO

Garden City, New York 11530

ISBN-0-8174-0771-5
Library of Congress Catalog Card Index 73-89737

Translated by E. F. Linssen, FZS, FRES, FRPS
from Blitzbuch

Printed by Biddles Ltd., Guildford, Surrey

Contents

Introduction

There are three golden rules for flash photography with any type of equipment:

1 Any type of blue flashbulb, or any electronic flash equipment, may be employed with black-and-white film, daylight type colour reversal film, or daylight or universal type colour negative film. The flash exposure received by the film depends on the distance from flash to subject, taken in conjunction with the flash output which will be found specified on the flashbulb carton or on the back of the flash unit.

2 Any type of blue flashbulb or electronic flash may be used with any type of camera, whether it be the simplest type, a between-lens shutter camera, a focal plane shutter type, or an automatic camera. Any possible difficulty is obviated by setting the shutter to a speed not faster than 1/30 sec. In the case of many automatic cameras this setting to 1/30 sec. is automatically made by switching over to the flash range. In the case of very simple cameras the slower of the two available shutter speeds, or the only available speed, according to type, operates at about 1/30 sec.

3 All types of flashbulb and electronic flash equipment may be used with any camera when set to the contact (sometimes indicated by the sign). Most cameras have only one flash connection with no contact changeover. Fortunately in such cases this is in fact the synchronization contact.

Other possibilities, using faster shutter speeds, and also the production of trick effects, are discussed later.

Construction of flashbulb

The essential components of a flashbulb are:

The *cap or base*.
Two *lead-in wires* which conduct the current through the glass seal into the interior of the bulb.
A *triggering filament* connecting the lead-in wires. This is extremely thin – a few thousandths of a mm – and so offers a high resistance to the current of about 1 ampere which is fed to it

through the electrodes. The filament thus becomes heated, incandescent, and finally melts.

A *priming paste* which is ignited by the filament and flares up to ignite the bulb filling.

The *bulb filling* which is a mass of very fine magnesium-aluminium or zirconium wire. The bulb interior is not, as commonly believed, a vacuum, but is filled with pure oxygen at above atmospheric pressure, which causes the metal to burn with high light output.

One or more coatings of *varnish,* which protect the bulb from splintering. In the case of the flashbulb most commonly used today, this layer is dyed blue. This "filter coating" adapts the colour of the light to an approximation of daylight.

A blue *indicator spot* on the inner surface of the bulb or on the bead of glass which holds the filament supports. This spot changes to pink should the bulb become useless through the penetration of air.

Construction of bulb flashgun

The basic components of a flash unit for expendable flash bulbs comprise:

The *holder,* into which fits the base of the flashbulb.

The *reflector,* which concentrates the light in the direction of the subject. Flash guns designed for flash cubes have no separate reflector, because each of the flashbulbs has its own reflector built in.

The *power unit*, see page 18.

The *foot,* which can be inserted into the accessory shoe of the camera or on to a flash bracket.

The *synchronizing lead* with its plug-in connection to the camera. The actual switch, which closes the flash circuit, is built into the camera and is operated automatically by the shutter. In many recent cameras and many of the modern type flash units designed to be used with them, the electrical connection requires no connecting lead, but is made through a contact on the accessory shoe.

The flashbulb *ejector.* This, as its name implies, ejects the used bulb from the holder. Removing spent bulbs from the holder with the fingers immediately after use can be painful.

As flashguns generally operate perfectly on any voltage between 3 and 30 volts, a simple dry battery should be adequate as power source. However the presence of resistance in the circuit delays firing or may even prevent it altogether – mainly in cases where the battery is already somewhat run down. Resistance of this kind is particularly liable to occur at all points of contact in the circuit: where the plug of the synchronizing lead enters the camera flash socket, or between the flash bulb contacts and those of the socket. This resistance can be still further considerably aggravated by dirt and oxidation at the metal surfaces.

Over and above this, the internal resistance of the batteries increases with age – precisely, it did increase in the batteries which were in general use some years back in flashguns. Today, the batteries employed are the modern alkali-manganese or mercury types (in some cases 1.5 V button cells).

Advantages of these modern batteries over the traditional dry cell include:

Excellent storage life, due to low self discharge.

Reliability even at extremely high and low temperatures.

Extremely small size.

Battery-capacitor circuits

Quite recently, direct triggering from a battery has come back into the picture as a result of the development of these new types of battery. Years ago another triggering system had been adopted which was not liable to failure through excessive oxidation. This was the capacitor flash unit, which I still personally regard as the best, and it comprised a circuit including an electrolytic capacitor, a high tension battery, a charging resistor and the flashbulb socket.

The circuit is so designed that with no flashbulb inserted no current at all passes. On inserting a flashbulb a current begins to flow through the resistor, the lead-in wires and the filament in the

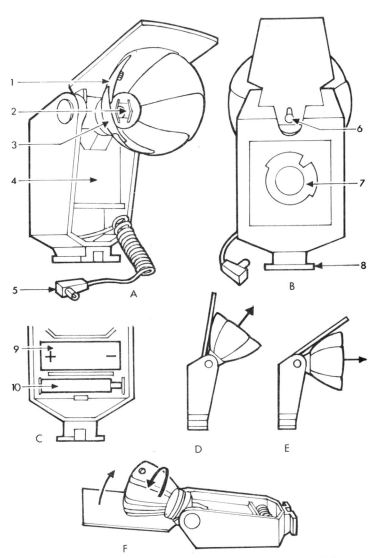

Small bulb flash. A, Front view. 1, Cover. 2, Bulb holder. 3, Reflector. 4, Battery chamber. 5, Connecting cable. B, Back view, 6, Bulb ejector. 7, Exposure calculator. 8, Accessory shoe fitting. C, Battery compartment. 9, Battery. 10, Capacitor. D, E, Flash head angled for bounced or direct flash. F, Reflector folded for stowing.

bulb, and so to the capacitor, which thus becomes charged. The only purpose of the resistor is so to reduce the flow of charging current as not to trigger the flashbulb. When the synchronizing contact in the camera short circuits this resistor/battery circuit, the charged capacitor is likewise short circuited through the flash bulb, and instantly – within about $1/1000$ sec. – discharges through the filament with sufficient current intensity to trigger it, even though it may have to overcome a few points of resistance in the circuit. To begin with, 22.5 V high tension batteries were used, and a capacitor of, usually, 100 µF capacity. Capacitor flashguns of this well tried type are still available today. In the course of time the tendency developed for both flashbulbs and flashguns to become smaller, and the capacitor flashguns, which were the most widely used type at that time, came to be equipped more and more with batteries of lower voltage – 15 volts – and capacitors of higher capacity – usually 200 µF.

Triggering circuits in flashguns which are built into cameras or which operate directly on the camera usually have a 6-volt battery and electrolytic capacitor of around 250 µF. This slight increase is not sufficient to compensate for the lower battery voltage. Consequently the 6-volt triggering systems are considerably less powerful. On the other hand the triggering reliability of flashguns has latterly greatly improved, and triggering occurs with a far smaller current. Nevertheless, where an extension cable more than 6 feet in length is employed between flashgun and camera, a battery voltage of 22.5 or 15 is advisable in the triggering circuit. Electrolytic capacitors may, incidentally, be either unipolar or bipolar. In equipment using a unipolar capacitor, the required battery polarity is indicated by "+" and "−". Where the capacitor is bipolar, the battery may be inserted either way in the flash unit – provided there are no other flash units coupled to it.

Batteryless flashcubes

The American Sylvania company use a new triggering system with their Magicube. This involves a special flash cube whose four component flashbulbs are triggered individually, without the use of a battery, by means of a firing pin. Unfortunately the Magi-

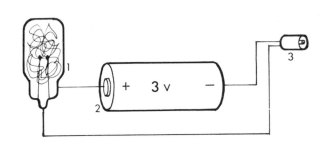

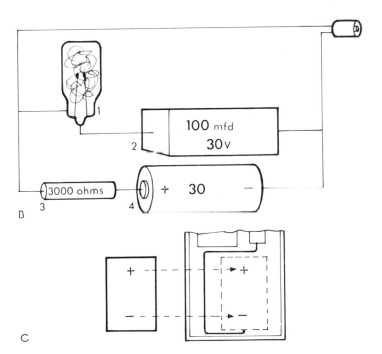

Flash construction. A, Simple circuit. 1, Bulb. 2, Battery. 3, Camera socket. B, Battery capacitor circuit. 1, Bulb. 2, Capacitor. 3, Resistor. 4, Battery. C, In most units the battery must be inserted the right way round.

cube can, so far, be used only in mounts which are built into particular camera models.

Types of bulb flashgun

Flashbulbs commonly in use today are made either with the standard capless or the AG-type fitting. Larger bulbs, more likely to be used by professionals, are supplied with various bayonet or screw caps. The socket of the flashgun has to be designed to fit the flashbulb base. Flash units built into the camera mostly have AG holders or else are equipped to take flash cubes. In general only one type of base will fit any individual flash unit. However there are also combination sockets which will accept both AG and capless flashbulbs.

As cameras today are equipped either with a flash socket or with a centre contact in the accessory shoe, there are available also two corresponding types of flashgun:

1 With flash cable connection for insertion into the flash socket on the camera.
2 With centre contact in foot. The connection is made when the flashgun foot is inserted into the camera accessory shoe.

Some types of flashgun are equipped with both flash cable and foot contact. This has the advantage that the flashgun can be attached to different camera types without any special adapter.
Some flashguns are provided with a plastic cover for attachment in front of the reflector as an additional safeguard, over and above the lacquer on the bulb, against any flying splinters of glass. This obviates any possible risk when photographing babies or small animals at close range.
An obvious precaution, also, is to enclose the whole reflector head in a plastic bag.
Some types of flashgun also have a built-in test lamp to provide a check on the functioning of both lamp and battery. For flashguns not so provided, special test lamps are available with sockets to fit the various flashbulb bases. These are simply inserted in place of the flashbulb.

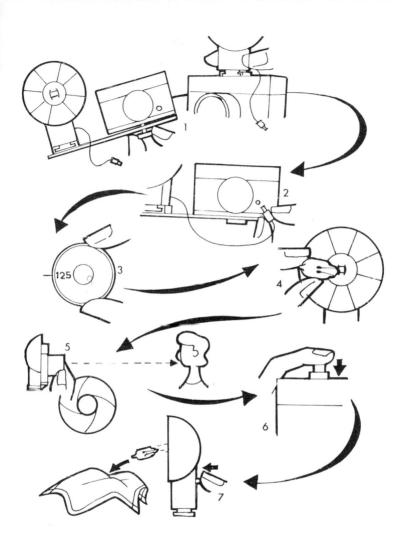

Using bulb gun. 1, Attach gun to camera. 2, Plug into camera socket. 3, Set shutter speed. 4, Insert bulb. 5, Focus and set aperture according to guide number and distance. 6, Press shutter release. 7, Eject flashbulb.

17

Construction of electronic flash unit

The basic construction of an electronic flash unit comprises:

1 Flash tube
2 Reflector
3 Connection to the camera (accessory shoe or flash cable or both)
4 Ready-to-shoot pilot light
5 Power pack

In smaller flash units the power pack is built into the main assembly; larger units have a separate power pack.
The power pack comprises:

1 Power source (battery, accumulator, or mains operated)
2 On-off switch
3 Vibrator or transistor circuit which takes over this function
4 Transformer
5 Rectifier
6 Capacitor or capacitors which store the flash energy.
7 Capacitor for the triggering impulse
8 Triggering inductance coil, which produces a high tension impulse.

The flash tube itself contains two electrodes, that is to say, two leads which enter the tube, which is not a vacuum, but is filled with gas (commonly xenon or a mixture of xenon and other gases). Normally the gas does not conduct electricity, and the electric charge stored in the capacitor cannot therefore of itself discharge through it. To enable this to happen, some of the electrons must first be set free at the electrode surface.
This is effected by setting in motion in some way a stream of electrons which serve as a conducting bridge within the tube, across which the energy stored in the capacitor can flow in concentrated discharge. The energy of this discharge is then converted into the light of the flash.
The requisite ionization, or rendering conductive, of the gas is effected by means of a high tension impulse. Produced by the dis-

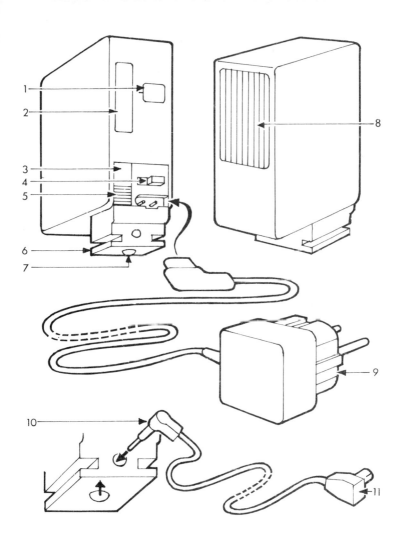

Electronic flash unit. 1, Film speed setting. 2. Exposure calculator. 3, Ready light. 4, On/off switch. 5, Manual firing switch. 6, Accessory shoe fitting. 7, Flash contact. 8, Diffuser window. 9. Charger unit. 10 Adaptor pin and base contact cut out. 11, Coaxial flash plug.

charge of the second – triggering – capacitor through its in-
duction coil, this impulse encounters the free electrons in the
most sensitive part of the xenon filling, setting them in rapid motion. The high voltage of this impulse releases the charge from
the capacitor, which stores energy at voltages of, as a rule, 350
or 500 volts. The energy flow of the flash discharge has quite a
high current value. It is therefore as well that it does not have to
pass through the synchronizing contact of the camera. Only the
primary impulse is admitted to this contact, and this, while being
of extremely high voltage, has low current strength.

How is it possible to produce in both the main capacitor and the
triggering capacitor so high an energy charge? How is the very
low voltage of a battery or accumulator transformed into so high
voltage a capacitor charge? When the unit is switched on, the low
voltage continuous current flows into an interrupter (or in these
days usually a transistor circuit) which converts the continuous
current (DC) to alternating current (AC). Continuous current cannot be transformed to a higher voltage (except by a relatively
massive rotary converter). In its new form of alternating current,
however, it can be "stepped up" in a transformer, but cannot
then, as alternating current, be used to charge a capacitor. The
high voltage current must therefore be converted once again to
continuous current – but this time at high voltage. That is the
function of the rectifier, which can take various forms. It acts as
a sort of one-way valve, allowing current to flow in one direction
only and so eliminating the to-and-fro action of the alternating
current. The main capacitor can be charged with this high-volt-
age direct current while a still higher voltage is created by taking
a voltage from a variable resistance across the main capacitor
and using it to energise the triggering inductance coil.

Types of electronic flash unit

The reflectors of electronic flash units, in contrast to flashbulb
reflectors, give a relatively high light concentration. Some types
can be adjusted so as to illuminate uniformly even the field of a
wide angle lens. Other units are provided with a diffusing disc
with the same object.

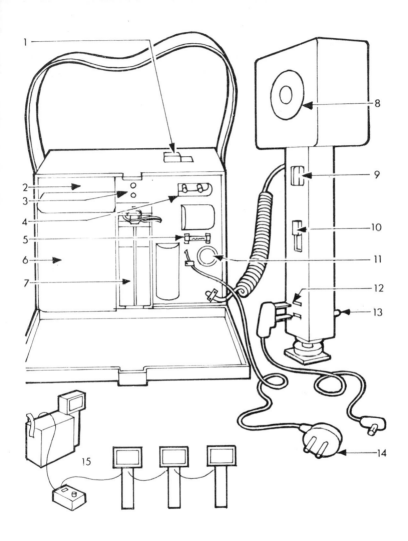

Larger electronic flash unit. 1, Full/half power switch. 2, Mains cable storage. 3, Mains plug parking. 4, Extension head connection. 5, Fuse. 6, Main condensers. 7, Battery. 8, Exposure calculator. 9, Ready light. 10, Switch for battery operation. 11, Voltage selector. 12, Sockets for camera connection. 13, Manual firing button. 14, Mains plug. 15, Many of the larger units allow several separate heads to be used.

Filters are supplied by some firms as accessories. Conversion filters for example, might correct the colour quality of the light to suit artificial light film. Very popular, too, and very useful, are UV absorbing filters. These are often built into the unit from the outset. The most up-to-date method is to provide the tube itself with a yellow coating which absorbs the ultra-violet.

There are many ways of equipping the unit with its power supply. A few inexpensive types are equipped for mains operation only. At the other extreme, there are dry battery units which cannot be operated at all from the mains. In between are units which may be used on either dry batteries or mains.

Various types of accumulator are used in the more expensive models. The accumulators can be recharged by connecting them to the mains through a cable which also permits direct operation of the unit from the mains. Lead-acid accumulators are giving way to nickel cadmium (NiCd) types, which are now the most widely used power source for electronic flash. They require very little attention. In some cases the user can himself change over the NiCd accumulators for a freshly charged set.

The time required to charge a discharged NiCd accumulator was, until recently, as a rule from 14 to 18 hours, but many electronic flash units are now supplied with rapid charging equipment. This will charge an empty accumulator to 45 per cent in 30 minutes. A vital component of every electronic flash unit is the neon pilot light which indicates that the capacitor is charged ready for shooting. The light output of the flash depends upon the state of charge of the capacitor. In the case of some strictly professional flash equipment the pilot lamp lights up only when the capacitor is fully charged. With other units it lights up when the capacitor has reached about 80 per cent of the fully charged voltage. As a rough guide it may be taken that charging is complete when the charging has been continued for the same length of time as it took for the pilot lamp to light up from switching on. However even by waiting for this extra time the extra light output of the flash at the most amounts to the equivalent of barely half a stop, and the circumstances must in each case decide whether such waiting is worth while. In the case of some very simple flash units the pilot lamp lights up prematurely, and the equivalent of a whole stop, or even more can be gained by waiting.

Many flash units today are provided with automatic control or power saver circuits. As soon as the capacitor becomes fully charged the drain on the accumulator is automatically switched off or reduced. When the voltage falls, of its own accord, or is reduced to zero by the firing of a flash, the recharge circuit is automatically switched on again. This renders it possible to carry the unit around for longish periods "at the ready" without undue drain on battery or accumulator. One manufacturer claims that its flash units can be kept switched on for fifteen minutes and yet consume only the energy needed for a single flash.

The latest development in the electronic flash sector is the so-called "computer flash" which automatically controls the light output to give correct exposure. A sensor, which is built into the flash head or into a separate attachment to it, measures the brightness of the flash-illuminated subject, and within a minute fraction of a thousandth of a second, in conjunction with a special auxiliary tube, quenches the flash discharge immediately the subject has received the right amount of light for correct exposure. (More about its practical use on page 46.)

The "quenching" tube used in this system constitutes what is, in fact, a second, dark-flash tube in parallel with the actual flash tube. Immediately its gases are ionized, at the command of the sensor, the remaining charge is dissipated through the lower resistance of the second tube and the current in the main tube ceases to flow. With the first of these computer flash systems only one particular stop could be used for any one film speed. In some newer types, there is a choice of two or three different stops and the units respond to indirect light.

It should be mentioned in passing that many electronic flash units, like some expendable flashbulb units, are provided with both flash lead and accessory shoe centre contact. A great many models can also be operated by pressing a button on the body of the flash head.

Shutter synchronization

If you are not sure of the shutter speeds at which you can use your flash equipment, set the shutter at $1/30$ sec. for first trials, and also whenever you want to be quite certain that the whole of the light output of a flashbulb will be effectively used. This applies to all flash equipment, whether automatic or manual, so far as concerns automatic equipment which can be switched over to manual operation. If your camera is an old model with no $1/30$ sec. setting, use the next slower speed.

Automatic cameras with no "manual range" usually have a special flash setting which automatically sets the shutter speed to about $1/30$ second.

The simplest cameras often have only one shutter speed. This may be safely used for flash. Some of the rather better cameras in this bracket however are provided with one fairly slow speed of about $1/30$ sec. and an additional rather faster one of around $1/100$ sec. In some cameras the faster speed is indicated by a sun symbol, the slower speed by a cloud and also a lightning flash symbol. There are models, too, which quite automatically change over to the slower speed when the flash unit, which is built into the top of the camera, is pulled out.

By far the greater part of all cameras have only one type of flash synchronization: the X synchronization. This obviates any difficulty of choice. Where there is more than one flash contact, or there is a lever to switch over from one type of synchronization to another, the standard setting to choose is always the X setting. This is indicated by the symbol X or $\frac{1}{2}$. If this rule is followed – irrespective of whether electronic flash or the popular types of flashbulb are used – good results are assured. However having harped ad nauseam on the absolute reliability of the standard rule, perhaps I may now say something of some special exceptions.

I personally use almost exclusively AG 3B and PF 1B flashbulbs and flash cubes with between-lens shutter cameras with X synchronization at a shutter speed of $1/60$ sec. ($1/50$ sec.). This results, it is true, in a loss of light equivalent to half a stop, but at the same time the effective exposure time is cut down to half. This results in a considerable increase in sharpness. Other flashbulbs – above all the larger types – should be used only with the $1/30$ sec. or even a slower shutter speed.

Theoretically, electronic flash units – used in conjunction with between-lens shutters and X synchronization – can be employed

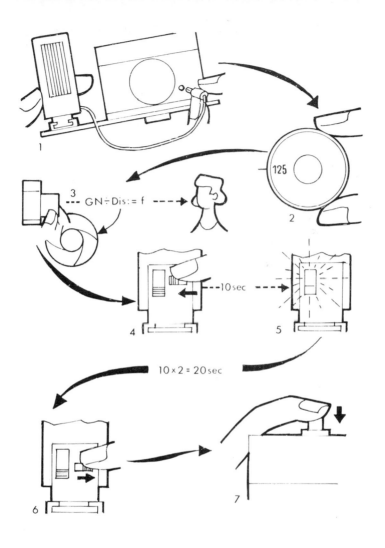

Using electronic flash. 1, Attach unit to camera and plug into camera socket. 2, Set shutter speed. 3, Focus, divide distance indicated into guide number and set aperture. 4, Switch on and wait for ready light to glow. 5, Wait for further equal time. 6, Switch off if only taking one shot. 7, Press shutter release.

with shutter speeds up to $^1/_{500}$ sec. For this, however, the shutter and synchronization must be in absolutely perfect adjustment. Most manufacturers of electronic flash equipment recommend as a precaution the use of a shutter speed around $^1/_{100}$ sec.

Many top-grade between-lens shutter cameras are provided with a change-over lever for setting to M synchronization. This was originally developed to enable flashbulbs to be used with faster shutter speeds – between $^1/_{50}$ and $^1/_{500}$ sec. In the way that old ideas are often to be found deeply rooted in peolpe's heads even after they have become obsolete, it is often said that flashbulbs should be triggered from the M contact, and electronic flash from the X contact. This view is perhaps a natural one for those of advancing age, but is nevertheless long outdated. Today both flashbulbs, and certainly electronic flash *belong* to X synchronization. X synchronization is essential to electronic flash: only with it can it illuminate the whole image field. But the use of flash lamps, too, with M synchronization is just pure extravagance: the faster the shutter speed, the more light goes to waste.

With the powerful flash bulbs of the PF 5 B, XM 5 B, No. 5 B, and Press 25 B types, at $^1/_{500}$ sec. only a bare quarter of the light is used as compared with that available at $^1/_{30}$ sec. with X synchronization. The remaining $^3/_4$ of the flash occurs before the shutter opens and after it has closed. With the smaller bulb, even more of the light goes to waste.

Admittedly in special cases of rapid movement in relatively strong ambient lighting it is helpful to use a higher power flashbulb with $^1/_{250}$ or $^1/_{500}$ sec. shutter speed in conjunction with M synchronization.

The smaller flashbulbs and flash cubes are definitely not to be recommended for use with M synchronization. At any shutter speed between 1 sec. and $^1/_{60}$ sec. half the light is just wasted. On the other hand, as already mentioned, the use of a $_1/_{60}$ sec. shutter speed cuts considerably the over-all effective length of the flash without serious loss of light. (I have myself successfully used Philips and Osram flashbulbs with $^1/_{60}$ shutter speed on X synchronization.) For the rest, there is no great hardship in abandoning the use of M synchronization, and, in fact, there are many cameras on which it is no longer available.

Turning to focal plane shutters, here, too, it would seem neces-

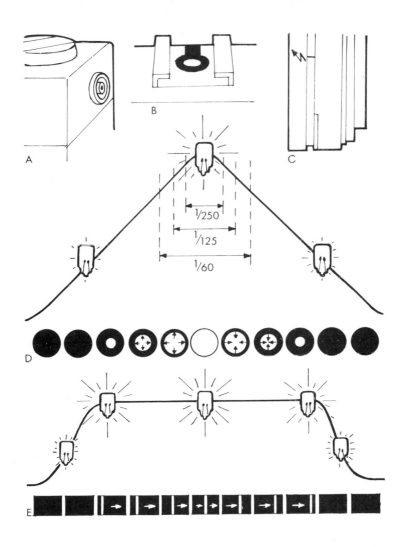

Flash characteristics. A, Coaxial socket in camera. B, Accessory shoe contact. C, Flash setting of shutter. D, Light from the ordinary bulb builds up to a peak and dies away. The slower the shutter speed, the more the light used. E, Special focal plane bulbs have long peaks to enable faster speeds to be used.

sary to correct a widespread misapprehension. It is frequently stated that focal plane cameras should be used only with special flash equipment designed for use with them. There are in fact special flashbulbs available for use with very high shutter speeds on focal plane cameras – but hardly anybody uses them. Otherwise, the statement is completely untrue. On X synchronization and $1/30$ sec. it is perfectly safe to use electronic flash, ordinary flashbulbs, and – if need be – the special focal plane shutter types as well. In any of these cases almost all the light output is utilized. But here comes a surprise: focal plane cameras are sometimes provided with two, or even three separate flash sockets. The second socket is usually not an M, but an F setting. The difference between the three connections lies in their delay periods. X synchronization triggers the flash immediately the shutter is fully open; M synchronization $1/60$, and F synchronization $1/300$ to $1/100$ sec. earlier.

As my own experience since 1954 has been with the Leica, with which therefore I am most familiar, I will use this as an example. Besides the X synchronization socket the M3 has a kind of F synchronization, designated by a lamp symbol. Using this socket I operate the AG and PFI flashbulbs not only at $1/60$, but also at $1/125$ and even at $1/250$ sec. I find this last speed very valuable because it gives me wonderful sharpness. The loss of light is of the order of two stops as compared with $1/30$ on F synchronization and four stops as compared with $1/30$ sec. with X synchronization.

With the large screw cap PF 60 flashbulb and my M3 I have taken pictures even at $1/1000$ sec. Admittedly under these conditions only about $1/40$th of the flashbulb light emission is utilized, but with the enormous light output of this flashbulb even this is by no means small.

Using X synchronization and electronic flash the shutter of the **Leica M3 should be set at $1/50$ sec, and of the Leicaflex at** $1/100$ sec. Other modern focal plane cameras in some instances likewise have highly satisfactory special synchronizing facilities for flashbulbs and electronic flash. As, however, I have no personal experience of these I must refer the reader to the – for the most part very detailed – instructions for use issued by the manufacturer.

For the rest, the synchronization of any camera can be tested

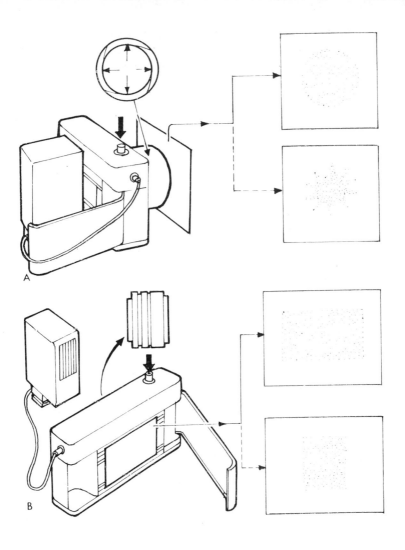

Testing synchronization. A, Between lens shutter. Fire flash through open camera back with bromide paper over lens in dimly lit room. Dark circle on paper indicates correct synchronization. Star or other shape indicates fault. B, With focal plane shutters remove lens and fire flash through lens mount with bromide paper in focal plane. Full image-area rectangle indicates correct synchronization.

without the need of a darkroom with the help of a 2 × 2 inch piece of enlarging paper, as follows:

Between-lens shutters: In a dimly lighted room hold the paper in front of the lens with the diaphragm fully open. Open the back of the camera, connect up the flash unit and place it directly up against the film guide. Then fire the flash by releasing the shutter. The paper should thus show a faint dark circle. Should it show instead a star pattern, this indicates that at the shutter speed chosen for the test the synchronization is not functioning as it should.

Focal plane shutters: Insert the paper in the film guide which would normally be occupied by the film. Remove the lens and direct the flash, by operating the shutter as before, from the front into the camera. The slight darkening which, without development, will appear on the paper must comprise a rectangle corresponding to the full format. Any smaller rectangle will indicate that the chosen shutter speed is too short to expose the whole format.

Maintenance and operation of flash equipment

There is not really much involved in the maintenance of the expendable bulb flashgun. Certainly unused flashbulbs should not be left in the flashgun for days at a stretch, or even, if it can be avoided, for a matter of hours, because this will mean that a continual weak current will be drained from the battery, thus slowly running it down, and at the same time reducing the reliability of firing of the flash. It can happen that the electrodes of the flash bulbs become somewhat oxidized. One way of minimizing this effect is to moisten the base briefly in the mouth.

Sticklers for hygiene will have to scrape the metal carefully with a knife! Plug and socket contacts can be kept clean by briefly inserting and withdrawing them three or four times.

The most damaging thing that one can do to electronic flash equipment is to put it away switched on. Dry batteries are rapidly destroyed; accumulators – even NiCd accumulators – suffer deep discharge, which is not good for them.

I have made a point of asking the various manufacturers of electronic flash equipment what they regard as essential maintenance precautions, of which the following is the essence:

Dry battery operated equipment

Electrolytic capacitors (used in most amateur units) need reforming (see below) from time to time.
If a mains supply is available, to form the capacitors during periods of disuse the unit should be connected up to the mains for half an hour to an hour every few weeks. Take the same precautions before putting it into operation after a longish period of disuse. Should no mains supply be available, switch on, without discharging the flash, for half an hour every few weeks during periods of disuse. There is no agreement among manufacturers as to whether, in all these cases, forming of the capacitor is expedited by additionally firing the flash 6 to 10 times.
The essentials underlying the forming of a capacitor are described in a service leaflet issued to customers by Bosch Elck tronic: "The electrolytic capacitor is best compared with a water barrel which is being slowly filled. If the barrel has stood empty for some time so that the staves have dried out, on re-filling some water will leak through, and this will continue until the staves have swollen again and the barrel has become watertight. Just as water is lost from the barrel, so after lengthy disuse of the capacitor a certain amount of current is lost on first switching on again, until it has regained its full storage capacity."

Lead accumulator operated equipment

Lead accumulators must periodically be topped up with distilled water. When charged, the plates must be just covered with liquid. It is important, too, to see that the accumulator is recharged immediately after a few flashes have been given. When not in use, the accumulator must be charged every few weeks. At least every four weeks it should be put on charge all night. So far as possible all the balls of the charge indicator should always be at the top when the unit is not in use.

31

NiCd accumulator operated equipment

NiCd accumulators, besides being small and handy, are above all dry, and are generally regarded as requiring no attention. This is not strictly true. One firm wrote to me very frankly: "These maintenance precautions (for lead accumulators) do not apply to NiCd accumulators, and this has led to the claim which is frequently made that these require no maintenance. Technically speaking this is perfectly true; but unfortunately it too often leads the user to assume that not only the accumulator but also the entire flash unit needs absolutely no attention. For this reason we no longer use the expression "maintenance free" in our technical literature and instructions. However we have still not been able yet to prevail upon our advertising text writers entirely to abandon it."

The essential requirements are:

1 Discharge of the accumulator down to the very last flash must be absolutely avoided.

2 Occasional overcharging – with a charging time of 14 to 18 hours – does no harm. However in general the charging time should not exceed 20 hours. (The very latest types of NiCd accumulator have a charging time of at most 2 hours.)

3 If the equipment is out of use for a time, it should be put on charge on the mains for half an hour to an hour every few weeks, and again, if possible, before being used again.

4 After using the flash unit put it on charge again at once.

5 Equipment which is out of use for a long period should be thoroughly recharged every 2 to 3 months.

The capacity of dry batteries and NiCd accumulators depends on the temperature. The light output falls with the room temperature:

at 0 °C by the equivalent of $1/3$ stop

at -10 °C by the equivalent of $2/3-1$ stop

at -20 °C by the equivalent of $1 2/3$ stop.

Likewise the number of flashes which can be obtained from a dry battery or a NiCd accumulator is reduced at 0 °C by 16 to 25 per cent, at -20 °C by up to 50 per cent.

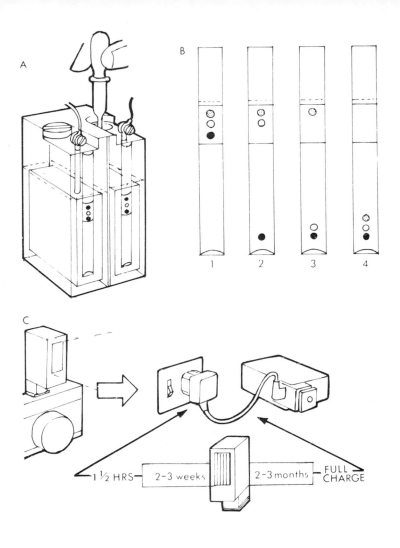

Battery maintenance. A, Topping up wet-cell battery, B, Charge indicator. 1, Full charge. 2, Part charge. 3, Recharging required. 4, Battery dead. C, Small electronic units should be recharged for 1½ hours every 2-3 weeks if unused. After 2-3 months a full charge is generally necessary.

Finally it should be emphasized that on no account should a flash unit be put away switched on, for this could easily result in severe permanent damage within a matter of 12 hours.

Accurate
Exposure
with Flash

The first pictures made by photography were taken with an exposure of eight hours. Today our shutters — with some exceptions — open for mere fractions of a second. The films of today are content with an extremely short exposure, or fast shutter speed.

If now we give a shutter exposure of $1/30$ sec. with X synchronization we are in fact dealing with a special case. For here the crucial factor is not the length of time the shutter is open, but the considerably shorter flash duration. Electronic flash, for example, has an average duration of around $1/1000$ sec.

A prerequisite is that stray light must not be obtrusive, and we therefore assume that we are photographing in a fairly dark room, and that the only important factor in the exposure is the flash. That being the case, it is immaterial whether the shutter speed used is $1/30$, $1/15$, $1/8$, or even $1/4$ sec. Things are quite different when a small flashbulb is used with a fast shutter speed — say $1/300$ sec. with M synchronization. The exposure time is then shorter than the duration of the flash.

Factors affecting exposure

Let us for the moment disregard the special case of M synchronization and consider only our justly popular $1/30$ sec. We must however bear in mind a further, vitally important difference between daylight and flash (and so far as that goes, any artificial light source). The illuminating power of flash alters with the flash-to-subject distance. We can do nothing about varying the distance of the sun from our daylight subjects. Instead, its light varies with the time of day and the weather. A flashgun always gives out the same light output.

In daylight, therefore, the factors controlling exposure are:

1 Film speed
2 Time of day and weather conditions
3 Lens aperture
4 Shutter speed

The exposure factors in flash photography (X synchronization, $1/30$ sec.) on the other hand are:

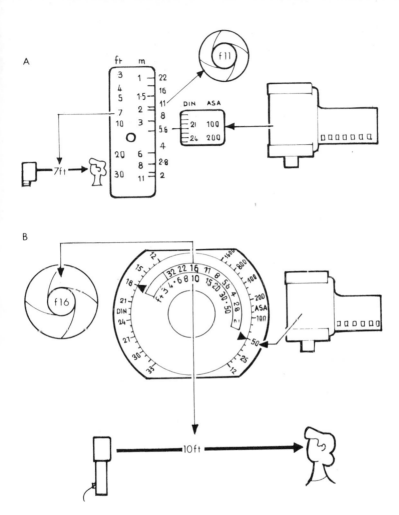

Exposure calculators. A, As you set the film speed, the distance scale moves. You read off the aperture required against the flash distance. B, The rotary dial works on a similar principle, the aperture numbers moving as you adjust the film speed.

1 Film speed
2 Light output of the flash tube or flashbulb
3 Lens aperture
4 Distance of the flash from the subject.

There are two ways of determining the correct exposure for the flash-subject distance, i.e. from a stop-distance table or calculator or from a guide number.

Stop and distance tables are printed on the back of cartons in which flashbulbs are packed. Abridged tables are sometimes engraved also on flashguns. There is then nothing to do but to look up in the table the stop corresponding to the flash-subject distance, taking account also, of course, of the film speed.

A rotating disc is the central feature of the stop calculator which is provided on many electronic flash units. The index mark on the disc is first set to the film speed. this automatically sets a range of distances against a range of stops – exactly as in the tables. Guide numbers, too, are printed on the back of flashbulb cartons (and as a rule, too, on stop calculators) – naturally for different film speeds. These provide a convenient means of calculating the required stop from the chosen subject distance: the guide number divided by the distance gives the required stop. Conversely by dividing the guide number by the stop we obtain the distance the flash must be from the subject. There are different guide numbers according to whether you work in feet or metres.

In the case of the very simplest cameras (box cameras) the stop cannot be varied. For such cases there are printed on the flash-bulb carton – and in some cases also on the back of the flashgun built into the camera – the range over which the most popular flashbulbs can be used.

Adjusting the normal exposure

The biggest source of exposure error is the use of a worn out battery or a run-down accumulator. This, as is well known, will result in failure of the flashbulb to ignite.

However there are a whole range of other possible reasons for incorrect exposures. Thus there may be a villain among manu-

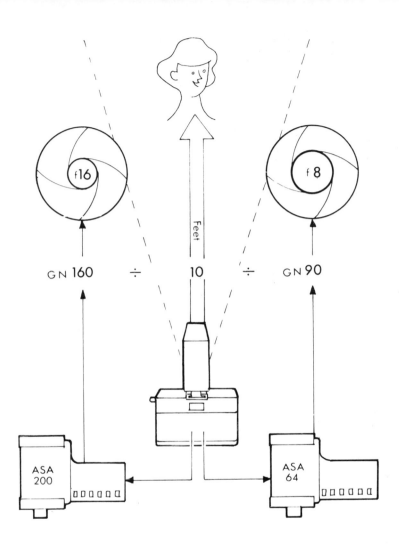

Guide numbers. The guide number varies with the film speed. Divided by the flash distance it gives the aperture to be used at shutter speeds using the full flash power.

facturers who gives inaccurate guide numbers. In the early days of electronic flash the widest use was made of this attractive possibility. Manufacturers, with loving care and much imagination, wrote up really inflationary data about their products. With flash equipment conforming to the DIN standards the DIN guide numbers can be safely relied upon to give correct exposure, at least in the middle of the picture. The standard does in fact permit a pretty high fall-off of illumination towards the edge of the subject. All this maybe sounds very dramatic, but there are people who find pleasure in photographing white walls and proving that some flashguns show an unacceptable fall-off of illumination toward the edges of the picture. As the main subject usually occupies the middle of the picture, however, such fall-off of intensity towards the edge has not the great importance which is sometimes attached to it.

Flashbulbs are generally mounted in wide angle reflectors which are of their nature suited to light large surfaces comparatively evenly. Moreover the high light output which is so surprisingly yielded by even the smallest of flashbulbs helps the manufacturer to give an honest guide number.

It can be, however, that reflectors – for the very reason that they so effectively spread the light over the room – do not exhibit quite the intensification factor which they properly should possess. Naturally this leads to underexposure. All exposure data for flash equipment are in Europe based on a reflector intensification of 4 (in USA, 5). In practice this means that the reflector is designed to concentrate four times as much light along its axis of reflection as would the naked flashbulb. It naturally follows that the naked flashbulb – with the reflector removed or blacked out – requires two stops more exposure or a reduction of flash-subject distance to one half.

In itself this degree of intensification is by no means too much to expect of a reflector, and in my opinion current flashbulb equipment fulfils this condition: some even exceed it. I would like to have been able to say that perhaps there was some error here. If, therefore, you are continually meeting with underexposure, try another flashgun. The little reflectors which are built into the very simple cameras occasionally fail to achieve the intensification factor prescribed by the standard. This however is not as bad as

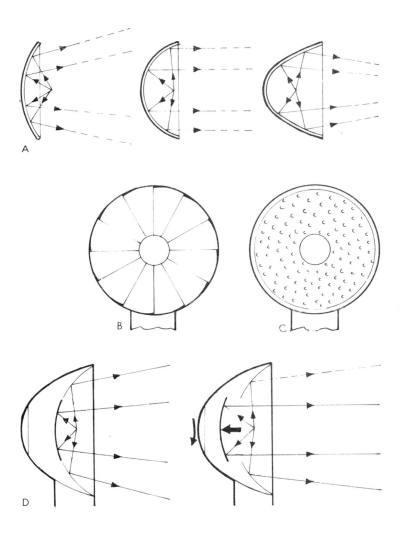

Reflector types. A, The shape of the reflector affects the nature of the beam. B, C, Bulb units may have folding or one piece reflectors with polished, satin-finish or dimpled surfaces. D, Some electronic units allow the tube to be moved to broaden the beam.

might appear, because in these cases the camera-subject distance range of the flash is stated on the camera.

In the USA an intensification factor of 5 is allowed for in specifying guide numbers for flash equipment. High efficiency special reflectors in some cases result even in far higher concentration. Practical tests have shown that a space factor has been incorporated in the guide numbers for electronic flash units and flashguns. Consequently the guide numbers hold "literally" only for living rooms of normal size with average light toned walls.

In using flash in small rooms with highly reflecting whitewashed or tiled walls the lens should be closed down by up to one stop. At the other extreme, flash photography at night outdoors, where there are no reflecting walls, requires about one stop wider aperture.

The same point holds good for large halls, where the walls are much too far away to have any effect. Rooms with dark wallpaper or extremely large rooms call for $1/2$ stop wider aperture.

It is interesting to note that the space factor is of much less importance in electronic flash photography. Whereas in an average room reflection from the walls increases the illumination of the subject as a rule by 100 per cent, their contribution in electronic flash lighting is only about 50 per cent. Electronic flash reflectors concentrate the light more effectively with the result that the surroundings are less illuminated. For this reason a much smaller space factor is incorporated in the guide numbers for electronic flash equipment.

The required exposure corrections resulting have been set out in the accompanying table (page 45).

It may seem somewhat surprising that this table shows a considerably greater aperture increase for negative film (both colour and black-and-white) than for colour reversal film. There are good reasons for this. Whereas exposures for colour reversal film have to be on the short side for contrasty subjects, exposures for negative films need to be more and more generous the higher the subject contrast. Portraits and animal pictures automatically become contrasty subjects when photographed by flash against a dark background.

Such subjects, moreover, must not be overexposed when using colour reversal film: in the case of negative film, on the other

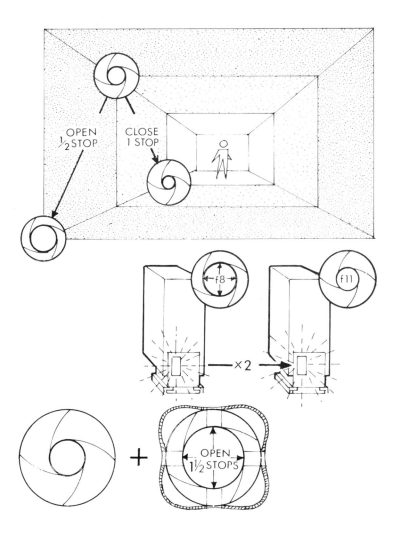

Exposure adjustments. Guide numbers indicate exposure required in average-sized rooms with medium-toned walls. In small or exceptionally light rooms, give one stop less exposure. In large or dark-walled rooms, give half a stop more exposure. When the ready light first glows, the capacitors are generally only 80 per cent charged. Full charge takes twice as long. Whenever in doubt, take an extra safety shot at $1^1/_2$ stops more exposure.

hand, if there is any doubt the lens should be opened up a little rather than risk under-exposure.

For the rest, the effect of room reflection is quite unnecessarily blamed for another trouble: strictly speaking the guide number holds good only down to a distance of 6 feet from the subject. At closer range the walls are so far away as compared with the subject that they cannot exert their normal effect in supplementing the subject lighting (further details on page 124).

One point should be noted: All that has been said about electronic flash equipment assumes that the flash is released only after the pilot lamp has been alight for some time. A further time should be allowed to elapse after it lights up equal to the time taken to light up after switching on. If the release is pressed immediately the pilot lamp lights up, the lens aperture should be opened up by something approaching a stop, because the capacitor is not yet fully charged. This applies to at least the greater proportion of equipment currently on the market.

Effect of subject on exposure

Before concluding this brief survey of exposure abnormalities there is one popular misapprehension which needs correction. It is repeatedly averred that a dark toned subject needs more exposure than a light toned one.

Using reversal film, a flash shot of a chimney sweep needs the same stop as one of a pastrycook. After all, there is no point in turning black into white, or even in lightening it. Conversely the last thing we want is to degrade whites.

Nor do we need, when using negative film, to underexpose the whites. Blacks, on the other hand, may safely be given double, and in exceptional cases even four times the normal exposure: that is, the aperture may be opened up an additional 1 to 2 stops. Blacks can in fact with the theoretically correct exposure come out so dark that there is no detail at all left in them. For this reason even with reversal film some slight concession has to be made for special cases.

In the chimney sweep we have an average subject – average in that besides the dark tones we have also light ones (face, back-

CORRECTIONS TO FLASH EXPOSURES

Room	Flash bulbs		Electronic flash	
	Reversal film	Negative film	Reversal film	Negative film
Medium size average tone living room	–	–	–	–
Outdoors at night (no light walls near at hand to reflect light)	Open up aperture 1 stop	Open up aperture 2 stops	Open up aperture $1/2$ stop	Open up aperture $1^1/2$ stops
In large halls, church interiors	Open up aperture 1 stop	Open up aperture 2 stops	Open up aperture $1/2$ stop	Open up aperture $1^1/2$ stops

(Note: Only for the usual flash distances of about 6–16 feet. No correction for large scale lighting set-ups.)

Room	Flash bulbs		Electronic flash	
Very large living rooms or rooms with unusually dark toned walls and furnishings	Open up aperture $1/2$ stop	Open up aperture $1^1/2$ stops	No correction or at most open up $1/4$ stop	Open up aperture 1 stop
Small, exceptionally light toned rooms (tiled bathrooms, modern kitchens)	Close down 1 stop	Close down $1^1/2$ stops	Close down $1/2$ stop	Close down 1 stop

ground). These light features must not be overexposed. If however we consider for example a black poodle taken so that its head occupies the whole field, then we may in fact overexpose even a reversal film to the amount of 1 to 2 stops. After all, in this particular case the picture includes no large areas of light tone which would risk becoming "washed out". The coat of a poodle is such a deep black that even overexposure is not likely to make it appear grey, but in fact will show off to better advantage the individual curls of the coat.

Also when the picture includes a white background which is

unimportant inasmuch as it will come out unsharp anyway, there is no objection to overexposure.

In case of doubt a flash shot can be taken strictly in accordance with the nominal guide number, then another with an aperture 1 1/2 stops wider – say f5.6 to f8 instead of f11. With this precaution nothing can really go wrong.

Exposure corrections with automatic flash

Automatic control of flash exposure is needless to say, of great advantage in that it obviates any need to bother with guide numbers or tables. However the question remains whether it is safe to rely blindly on the various flash automation systems in all circumstances. Or is it permissible under certain conditions to make small corrections. Let us therefore make a closer examination of the various basic types of automatic flash.

In one system – which is built into the camera – the mere act of focusing adjusts the stop. The coupling between focusing mechanism and iris diaphragm comes into action immediately the camera is changed over to the flash range. The guide number corresponding to the type of flash and film speed have of course to be preset on the camera. All that remains is to set the focus to the subject distance, and the iris diaphragm automatically adjusts itself to give the correct exposure for that distance.

However deviations from standard reflection conditions are not automatically compensated by this type of camera: outdoors at night, for example, as with any other camera, a larger stop must be used or alternatively the camera set to a lower guide number.

The other type of automatic flash system operates with a light sensitive sensor. This may be built into the camera, as in various "instant picture" cameras. These exercise direct control on the exposure time. The shutter closes immediately the flash bulb has emitted sufficient light to give the correct exposure. The rest of the light emitted just goes to waste.

For some time now, however, there have been available also electronic flash units with a built-in sensor. These have become known as computer flash units. As do the instant picture cameras, these also have a sensor which measures the quantity of

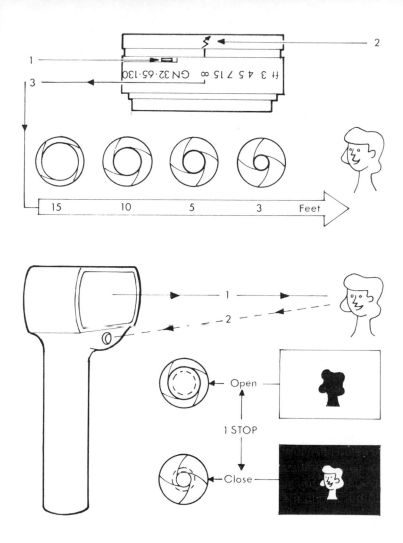

Automatic flash. 1, Guide number indicator. 2, Flash symbol set to focusing index mark. 3, Aperture varies with setting of focusing scale. Self'quenching flash has sensor reading light reflected from subject. Adjustments to recommended aperture may be required for unusual subjects.

light which is reflected back by the subject. As soon as this quantity reaches the required value, the light from the flash tube is quenched.

The stop to which the diaphragm is set is decided by the film speed: this then remains unaltered regardless of whether, according to type, the subject is 16–23 feet away from the camera or as close as 2 feet. Medium speed films – say, of 50 ASA – call for a stop of about f4.

For the rest: By means of a simple trick, computer units can also be adapted to close-up use. All that is needed is to interpose a dark filter over the sensor. It is of course necessary to close down the lens correspondingly to a considerably smaller aperture. The range of automatic operation is considerably shortened, but against this we can approach much closer to the subject. The stop required, and the new range over which the automatic operation functions, must be determined by trial exposures.

More recent equipment is equipped with a sensor diaphragm. This offers the advantage of a choice of three stops – e. g. f4, f5.6 and f8. (For indirect, or "bounce", lighting using computer flash, see page 87). It is thus possible to exercise control over the depth of field.

All computer flash units automatically take into account the effect on exposure of any contributions made to the lighting by the presence of any reflecting surroundings. On the other hand with this automatic control any exceptionally bright or dark feature in the subject can throw the picture completely out of balance. Any bright reflection can make the picture as a whole too dark, and this will have to be corrected by opening up the stop.

Consequently whereas – as already explained – with non-automatic equipment little or no adjustment to the exposure should be made in respect of exceptionally dark or light areas of the subject, it is essential, when using automatic flash equipment, to take them into account.

The requisite corrections can be illustrated by four examples:

1 *Subjects which are exceptionally dark-toned throughout* – e. g. the "black cat in a coal cellar" Here the sensor is deceived by the predominance of dark, and gives a correspondingly excessive exposure. However this does not matter, because the

Shot against a non-reflecting background, the fencer is well illuminated by the frontal flash and his position is well illustrated. The high viewpoint enables the placing of the legs and arms to be indicated clearly.

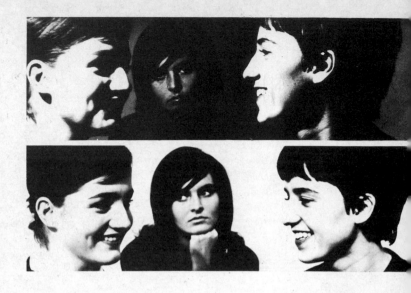

Subjects in depth are differently rendered according to the distance of the flash. For the top picture above the flash was positioned fairly close to the subjects. Consequently the closer figures are overlit and the farther figure underlit. For the lower picture, the flash was placed much farther back so that the fall-off effect was less pronounced. Lighting thus became more even throughout the depth of the subject.

Opposite: A similar effect is obtained even with a single model, in this case a Japanese doll, photographed indoors. When the flash is used at close range, reflections from surrounding walls, ceiling, etc., have a disproportionately small effect. When the flash distance is increased, reflections help to balance the lighting.

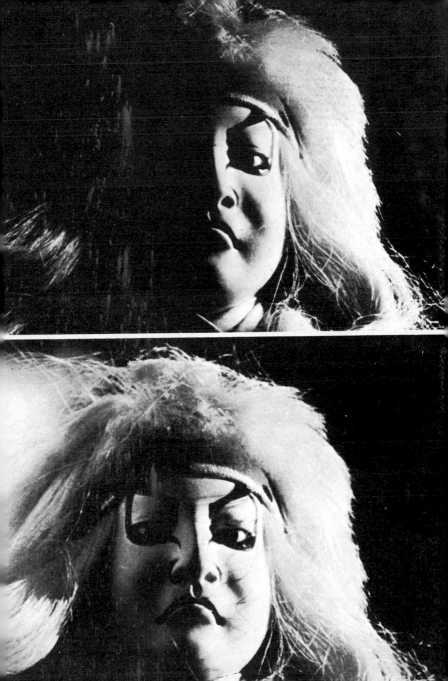

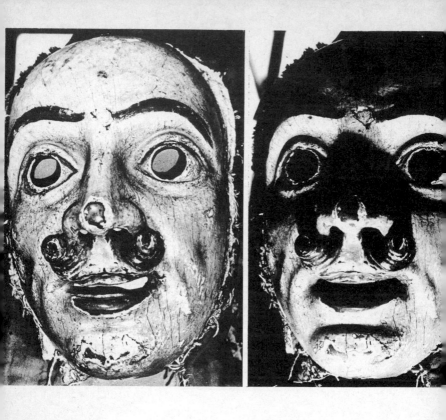

The angle of the lighting has a considerable effect on the features. Lit slightly from one side with frontal fill-in, this mask presents a reasonably normal appearance in the picture on the left. Lit from below as if from footlights, a much more dramatic appearance is obtained in the picture on the right.

Texture is shown much more readily by angled lighting than by light directed entirely from the front. The top picture gives little idea of the depth of the object while the side lighting of the picture below throws heavier shadows and emphasises the irregular nature of the surface. Backlighting is used effectively on the left to show the construction and also to provide an effective pattern picture.

Positioning a single flash off the camera to the right has given reasonable modelling and separated the head adequately from the background.

This golden bust is under glass and direct lighting is impracticable, because it would cause multiple "hot-spot" reflections. Indirect flash from a large reflector provided a more acceptable result.

When shooting at close range the lighting can be relatively weak. Even the smallest electronic flash units can cover subjects like these if placed within one or two feet (0.3 to 0.6m) and still allow the lens to be stopped well down—*Peter Rowe, Max Hess.*

over-all dark subject can quite well bear a certain amount of such overexposure, because there is no light-toned detail which would be liable to be burned out. Therefore: despite all – no stop correction!

2 *A small black area against a light background* such as a dark spot on the pure white of a snowman. Here the sensor sees too much white and gives too short an exposure. Open up the lens one stop.

3 *Subjects which are white against white,* such as a bride, dressed entirely in white, with white bouquet, against the gleaming background of Mont Blanc. Here, the intense white "saturates" the sensor prematurely. Open up the lens one stop to avoid too thin a negative or a degraded white in a colour slide.

4 *A white spot against a black background,* e. g. a black rabbit against the night sky nibbling at a white cabbage leaf. The sensor is now overinfluenced by the prevailing dark, and overexposes accordingly. Close the lens down one stop.

It may be interesting here to summarize the results of a few tests made with various computer flash units. There is, however, no suggestion that any general conclusions are to be drawn from them.

1 At relatively long distances, e. g. 13–16 feet, the automatic system can easily lead to underexposure. In such circumstances it is better to revert to manual control.

2 With very close subjects, on account of the extremely short flash durations involved, some films exhibit a colour shift towards the blue. In my own experience this has not proved objectionable. On the contrary, the effect was one of better colour separation and increased contrast.

3 With side lighting, glancing light and so forth (page 100) it is safe to use the automatic control. Here the tendency is rather towards over than underexposure.

4 Automatic control can also be used where several computer flash units of modern type are connected together and simultaneously fired.

The best working distance for most subjects is between 5 and 6^1/$_2$ feet.

Some notes on flash exposures

Among my slides is a portrait of a dancer from Ghana. Notwithstanding the speed and vivacity of the dance, the detail of the face is perfectly sharp. However the dancer was wearing a golden earring. This sent out a brilliant reflection, which made a very long, bright streak right through the middle of the picture.

So the question arises: Do flashbulbs and electronic flash give considerably longer exposures with bright subjects than with dark ones? Admittedly a somewhat strange question! Nevertheless the answer must be: Yes, they do!

Neither the electronic flash tube nor the flashbulb radiates the same intensity throughout the whole flash duration. From the instant of triggering, the intensity of the flash increases up to a maximum, which is termed the peak intensity. It then falls again to zero. This can be shown diagrammatically in curves, termed intensity time curves, or in oscillograms. These diagrams – often of fascinating shape – are like mountain peaks, rising sharply on one side and falling more gradually on the other. The light intensity does in fact usually increase rapidly to peak value, at which most of its output is achieved, finally dying away considerably more slowly. Why trouble to explain all this? We are sometimes told that flashbulbs have a flash duration which exposes the film for $1/80$ to $1/100$ sec. Electronic flash tubes are assumed to have flash durations of $1/500$ to $1/1000$ sec. In fact, some flash units have a flash duration as short as $1/5000$ sec. With many studio electronic flash units on the other hand the exposure extends to $1/200$ sec. Now this flash duration, which is specified as the effective photographic exposure time, is shorter than the total time taken by the flashbulb to burn out, or the electronic flash completely to discharge. There is some justification for saying that within the over-all time there are long periods during which the amount of light radiated is so small that it cannot possibly have any effect on the exposure. Consequently the effective flash duration commences only at the instant at which the light intensity has attained a certain minimum value. The effective flash duration consequently extends from this instant until the time when the intensity has again fallen to the initial accepted minimum value. In the case of flashbulbs, the minimum intensity is usually regarded as one half, and in the case of electronic flash one tenth of the peak intensity.

The build-up and falling off periods, during which there is but very small light emission – especially the falling off period following the flash – have no effect at all on the exposure. At least, in theory. In practice it confronts us with such problems as that of the glistening earring.

Take, for instance, the case of a subject in rapid motion comprising a grey area, a white area, and a polished surface which reflects the flash. As the flash dies away the residual light emission falls to a point at which the grey surface reflects too little light to affect the film. The white surface, as well as the polished surface, are at this point still reflecting enough light to continue exposing the film. Meantime the flash emission falls still further, until the white surface likewise falls below the threshold reflection value. There then remain only the brilliant reflections in the polished surface capable of affecting the film – and this continues to the bitter end of the flash discharge.

The result of all this is that the grey surface will probably appear sharp in the picture despite the subject movement. The white surface will show a slight movement blur, while the reflections in the polished surface will leave a long, comet-like streak behind the main image.

The conclusion to be drawn from this is that subjects in rapid motion of low contrast and not too light in general tone have a better chance of being recorded perfectly sharp than subjects which are extremely light in tone or even exhibit direct specular reflections. The only solution is to use the fastest permissible shutter speed, but with many focal plane shutters no fast speed can be used.

Flash-on-
Camera
Techniques

It is frequently claimed that frontal flash is at best a makeshift. That really effective pictures and frontal flash are mutually contradictory! Certainly, anyone who intends to take up flash photography seriously would be well advised to provide himself with an extension cable to enable him to place the flash at a distance from the camera.

Nevertheless, even frontal lighting can serve a useful purpose in picture composition. It ensures, for instance, that in portraiture the face is smooth and free, or at least nearly free, from wrinkles or creases. There is no better way of suppressing wrinkles, warts, and other facial blemishes in portraiture than by using only lighting from the same direction as the camera. Photographically speaking this is a kind of rejuvenating process. Admittedly, the face will lack modelling; it appears flat, and sometimes too broad.

Eliminating background shadows

The most objectionable feature of frontal lighting however, is the formation of a dark edge of shadow. This is in fact the shadow of the subject on the background, and appears as a dark rim adjacent to the edge of the subject. It should be emphasized that in the case of a flash unit built into the camera this dark edge is comparatively narrow, and correspondingly unobtrusive. The reason for this is that in this case the lens and flash source are very close together. The shadow becomes wider and very much more obtrusive when the distance between flash and camera is increased – as for example when the flash is mounted on a flash bracket attached to the camera.

In point of fact all such shadow edgings are more or less objectionable whether they be narrow or wide. Fortunately there are ways of mitigating them, or even of entirely suppressing them. And it is in these that lie the potentialities of pictorial composition by way of – or in spite of – frontal flash lighting. Here are four quite simple tricks which can be strongly recommended. With their aid the pictorial effect can be improved almost beyond belief.

1 If the flash is mounted on the upper part of the camera, the shadow on the background will "embellish" with a shadow edge

Background shadows. A, Flash close to side of camera throws deep shadow on one side of figure. B, Flash above lens throws shadow all around figure. C, Remedy in such cases is to move model away from background. D, E, Alternative remedies are to place model against open doorway or window.

the lower extremities of the subject. In a half-length portrait, for example, these dark edges will be seen beneath the nose, chin, and arms. If the flash comes from the left hand side of the camera a dark rim will outline the right hand side of the subject, and of course conversely. Care should therefore be taken in each case to direct the camera – with its flash – in such a way that the shadow does not lie adjacent to a full or semi-profile. When it lies against the back of the head, such a shadow is much less objectionable.

2 Far better is to choose a dark background for the subject. Against a light toned wall the black outline shadow is particularly objectionable, but against a black background it becomes completely invisible. This offers a complete solution to the problem.

3 Bear in mind particularly that the subject does not have always to be right up against the background. Also that even a light wall becomes quite dark as soon as it is taken far enough back from the subject. With the light thus seeping away with the background distance, the dark shadow rim disappears into the general blackness.

4 Place your "model" against an open window or a house or balcony door: the shadow will then disappear out in the open space. So long as your flashbulb is not too powerful, and you are shooting from three feet from an open door, there is no need to use so small a stop. There will then be a good chance that the sky or landscape background will be rendered fairly light in the picture. If need be, the flash can be dimmed with a handkerchief held in front of it, thus enabling the diaphragm to be opened up still further.

Dealing with the "red eye" effect

Poets have sung of "sparkling eyes", but never of the fact that our pupils glow red. It is only since the coming of colour photography that this has become a matter of general knowledge. Maybe the reader has already come up against transparencies which show the effect. It gives portraits a quite uncanny look, with the bright, fiery red spot gleaming from the pupils. The effect is exclusive to flash pictures.

The red glow comes in fact by reflection from the red surface – the retina – which forms the back of the eye. It is scarcely ever observed except in photographs, and then only provided three conditions are fulfilled:

1 Frontal lighting.
2 A very low level of general lighting – preferably complete darkness – so that the iris remains fully open.
3 Brief exposure (slight underexposure).

The surest antidote lies in removing the flash unit from the camera and using it to give not strictly frontal illumination but a slightly side, top, or under lighting.
However we have to agree that it is not always possible to separate the flash from the camera. There remains only one possibility: avoid darkness! Even if you are anxious to preserve the Christmas or birthday atmosphere in the flash photograph, switch on all the normal room lighting.
But if the picture has to be taken out of doors at night, at least the subject should avoid looking directly into the camera.

Retaining normal lighting effect

It is not possible in a normal flash photograph to reproduce the general lighting effect in the room, even when it is lit by bright tungsten lamps. Only by setting the shutter to a much slower speed than $1/30$ sec. can the room lighting have any noticeable effect on the picture. There is no possibility that the presence of such lamps may become obtrusive in the normal flash shot. The only way in which their presence can be even detected is when they themselves actually appear in the picture: maybe a candle flame, the glowing filament of a clear glass bulb, or the glow of a fluorescent tube. These may just register on the film. So far as I am concerned – and this I must emphasize – it doesn't bother me in the least if the actual light sources appear in the picture. On the contrary, I find that they lend a certain atmosphere to the picture. The warm, reddish artificial light makes a quite striking contrast against the cooler lighting of the flash.

Needless to say, the extent to which such light sources are recorded in the picture depends on the shutter speed chosen, as well as the stop. The use of a wide aperture in this connection naturally assumes that the flash itself will be appropriately dimmed – either by the handkerchief method (page 72) or, if this is practicable, by removing the reflector.

The most convenient way is probably the use of indirect, or "bounce" flash (page 84), especially when it is desired to record in the picture to full effect such weak lighting sources as candle flames. (In any case the actual flash exposure should be kept to a minimum – the equivalent of one stop below normal – otherwise the flash will destroy the whole effect.)

I always take care, incidentally, to include the powerful stage spotlights in theatre pictures. Flash shots outdoors at night are made specially effective by the inclusion of such things as illuminated advertising signs and car headlamps.

Extra lighting effects and open flash

The open flash method – that brings me back to my very first flash photograph! And that's a long time ago! In those days synchronized cameras were still a rarity. Even if my camera had been synchronized it would not have been of much use to me, for flash-bulbs were still scarcely obtainable. With my Boy-Scout troop I had been haunting an undeveloped stalactite cave, and it stands to reason that we wanted to photograph the interior. So we had to use flashpowder – a flash technique which was even then as dead as the dodo, but whose relics we had unearthed.

The space had to be completely dark, which with our cave presented few difficulties. The shutter, set to time, was then opened, and the flash fired. Immediately the flash had died away the shutter was closed. In these days it is a relatively quick and simple matter to fire electronic flash or flashbulbs by the "open flash" method. If the equipment has no manual release I simply short circuit the plug on the synchronizing cable with a paper clip or a ball point pen.

With flash powder, firing the flash was a regular ceremony. From the flash powder receptacle, hung up in some convenient place, trailed a paper streamer, the end of which had to be lit with a match. The flame ran up the paper "fuse": Everyone shut their eyes in expectation of the brilliant flash. And then... It came! Or it didn't! In our cave, we were lucky.

In the foregoing section it has been shown how it is possible with advantage to utilize the existing general lighting sources in a flash picture, and that it is often advisable, to this end, to use a slower shutter speed than $1/30$ sec. If the exposure time is still further prolonged, as the length of the shutter exposure is increased, more and more of the general lighting becomes recorded on the film, and eventually we inevitably reach a point where the whole effect of the general lighting is registered. With floodlighted sports arenas and stage productions this already occurs with relatively short exposures, because the general lighting here is very intense.

Even at shutter speeds of $1/30$ or $1/60$ sec. some evidence of the general lighting is – often unintentionally – to be seen. This naturally depends also on the intensity of the flash. The weaker this is, the more the stop must be opened up, making it easier for the general lighting to record on the film. The general tendency now is by use of the shortest possible shutter speed and a high power flash unit to suppress recording of the general lighting to the point where only the spotlight itself is visible. On the other hand the general lighting can of itself give quite attractive effects.

On one occasion I took the opportunity of taking pictures at a performance of the Jugoslav National Ballet, and used a $1/5$ sec. shutter speed for a flash shot of a dancer executing a rapid pirouette about her own axis. With the stage brilliantly illuminated and a light toned background the entire background appeared bright in the transparency naturally in the warm tone of the artificial lighting. In a way the result was a blend of two pictures – a sharp, cold toned flash picture of the dancer superimposed on the unsharp, reddish yellow background of the stage lighting.

Since then I have used this technique many times with success. This type of picture is of its nature highly informative: On the one hand it gives a flash record of the essential subject in minutest detail. On the other the stage lighting, in conjunction with the longish exposure, traces the source of the movement. The two records however are in striking contrast in both sharpness and colour. The colour contrast can of course be still further emphasized by filtering the flash blue or green.

Under ordinary living room conditions, an exposure of at least a second or so will be needed to obtain such an effect.

Contrast effects of this kind are however only really successful provided the flash does not too strongly illuminate the background. In practical terms this means that the background should be at least as far behind the main subject as the flash is in front of it.

Fill-in flash in daylight

When – years ago – I first began to hear talk of fill-in flash in daylight photography, I regarded it as a clever advertising stunt. In the meantime I have had ample opportunity to convince myself that this early judgment was ill founded. I humbly ate my words and was forced to admit that fill-in flash in daylight outdoors can be one of the most interesting photographic techniques, especially as modern refinements have made it so simple to combine these two types of lighting – flash and daylight – in pictorial composition.

It is interesting to note that this combined use of flash and daylight in outdoor photography can be made to serve two fundamentally different, and to a degree even opposite functions.

In sunlight, its aim must be to soften the subject contrast. Lovely as are the delicate golden rays of the sun, they are also responsible for deep black shadows which can completely spoil the picture, no matter what the subject. A portrait is just as liable to suffer as a work of art. Up to a point, in black-and-white photography the shadow problem can be dealt with by overexposure. Colour photography on the other hand calls for the assistance of flash, which relieves the darkness of the shadows and so reduces the overall subject contrast.

In dull weather there would be no point in thus reducing the subject contrast, for in dull diffused light the subject already has too little! Dull weather pictures are inevitably lacking in brilliance. Nevertheless we can still call on the services of flash by way of substitute for the sun's rays which refuse to break through the

clouds just when they are wanted. Here its purpose is not to reduce contrast but to increase it.

In sunshine, the sun itself is as a rule used as the main light
source, the flash serving only as an auxiliary source. In dull
weather the reverse is the case. The flash takes over the main role
and relegates the dull daylight to mere fill-in duties.

In the annexed table are summarized all the potentialities of flash
plus daylight.

For eliminating colour cast I prefer to use clear flashbulbs. The
contrast between the resulting intrinsically warm toned foreground and the colder background gives the pictures a "certain
something" which I find exceptionally attractive. As clear flashbulbs are not always readily available today, I just scrape off the
varnish from a blue bulb with a knife. It comes off relatively easily.
It is true that this varnish coating has also the purpose of safe-
guarding the glass from splintering; to ensure, therefore, that no
one gets hurt by flying splinters the flash head should be protected with a transparent plastic envelope. Thus I find it quite satisfactory to use a plastic raincoat when photographing babies or
other sensitive subjects from close up with unprotected flash
bulbs.

Exposure for daylight flash fill-in

To begin with, I would not recommend the conventional, univer-
sally publicized method of determining the relationship between
the daylight exposure and the flash fill-in. Only for the sake of
completeness is it referred to here. Besides, why make things too
simple when in fact they are complicated?

Using the exposure meter we set the camera to the stop required
for a shutter speed of $1/30$. or better $1/60$ sec. The guide number is
then divided by this stop value to give the distance at which the
flash must be placed from the subject.

Any apprehension that this might lead to overexposure, because
the sunshine and flash exposures are additive, is entirely un-
founded. Since outdoors in the open there is no room reflection
the flash exposure is inadequate anyway to the extent of $1/2$ stop
(electronic) to 1 stop (flash bulb). This is of no account when only

FLASH PLUS DAYLIGHT EFFECTS

Flash effect desired	Type of daylight
Relief of cast shadows	Sunshine
Suppression of blue cast	Sun at midday
Suppression of reddish-yellow cast	Sunrise or sunset
"Warming up" of general cold tone	Overcast sky; in the shade on a sunny day
Suppression of coloured reflections (e. g. green reflection from grass or foliage)	Mainly sunshine
Sunshine effect. Brightening up a flat subject	Overcast sky, dull day, in the shade on a sunny day
Darkening an over-light background. Flash to illuminate foreground only	On cloudy days; in sunshine when flash is close to subject
Background to be rendered deep black even in bright daylight. Flash to illuminate foreground only. (Effective only with close-ups)	In any weather. (Flash must be very close to the subject)
Suppression of wrinkles and facial blemishes. Youthful appearance in portraits	In any weather
Fill-light for silhouettes. Figures at window or in shade against light background, which would otherwise come out too dark	In any weather
Fill light for contre jour subjects	In sunshine outdoors or at the window

fill-light is involved, and it is a question only of relieving shadows, and not of giving full exposure to the picture. In dull weather, certainly, when the flash is used as a substitute for sunshine, the flash exposure should of course be given full effect. In this case the figure taken as basis for the calculation should be, not the

70

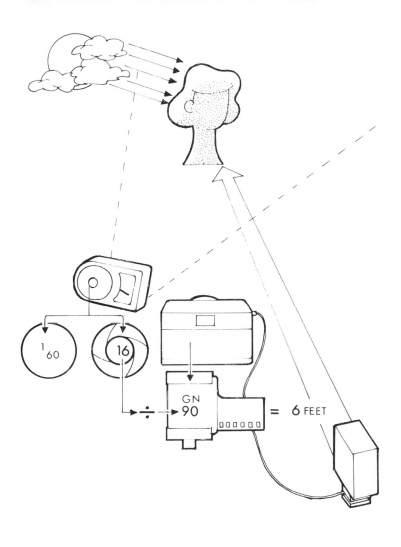

Fill-in flash. Read exposure required for daylight at suitable shutter speed for flash. Divide aperture into guide number to obtain required flash distance. Use extension flash cable if required.

stop set, but one stop smaller. This is readily possible, because in dull weather the flash distances are correspondingly long. But let's forget about stupid calculations! In practice only one thing matters: the range of distance over which we can use our flash. This depends on:

1 The light output of the flash unit
2 The brightness of the daylight
3 Within certain limits, the shutter speed set.

Broadly speaking the range is not dependent on the film speed. Is that surprising? At first glance one would think that when flash is used as a fill-light the range, as is the case in the ordinary way whether at night outdoors or in an indoor shot, will be the greater the faster the film. Until practical experience taught me better I, too, was firmly under this mistaken impression. But there is one thing that has to be borne in mind: as soon as a faster film is used, for a daylight shot the lens must be correspondingly stopped down. As a result, the increased range which might have been expected from the higher film speed is negatived by the smaller stop. the only exception to this is where a faster shutter speed is used instead of stopping down.

The diagram on page 73 shows the ranges of a number of different flashbulb and electronic flash units under good and bad weather conditions.

The requisite stop must be determined with an exposure meter. (Note: The guide numbers quoted for electronic flash units in all cases relate to a film speed of 18 DIN or 50 ASA).

Within the lightly shaded ranges there is a very high level of flash fill-lighting, or, in the case of dull weather, a "sunshine" effect. On the other hand in the dark shaded zones the fill-lighting is still clearly apparent.

i can well appreciate the strong temptation on occasion to approach considerably nearer to the subject with the flashgun. Nevertheless, if it is brought nearer than is indicated by the shaded zones there will be a risk of overexposure.

In these circumstances a white handkerchief can help. Placed, folded, in front of the flash it reduces its intensity. As a rough guide, a single thickness gives about one stop reduction, a dou-

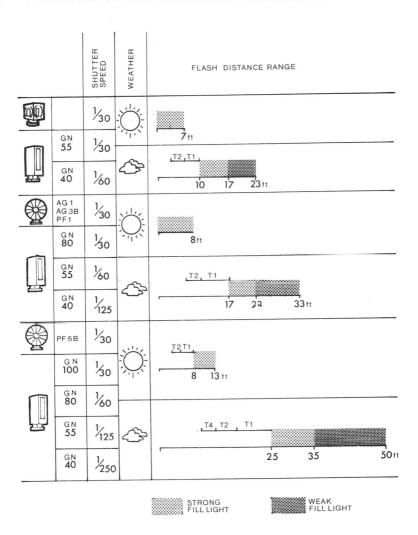

		SHUTTER SPEED	WEATHER	FLASH DISTANCE RANGE
		1/30	☀	7 ft
	GN 55	1/30	☁	T2, T1
	GN 40	1/60		10 17 23 ft
	AG 1 AG 3B PF 1	1/30	☀	
	GN 80	1/30		8 ft
	GN 55	1/60	☁	T2, T1
	GN 40	1/125		17 23 33 ft
	PF 5B	1/30	☀	T2 T1
	GN 100	1/30		8 13 ft
	GN 80	1/60		
	GN 55	1/125	☁	T4, T2 T1
	GN 40	1/250		25 35 50 ft

▦ STRONG FILL LIGHT   ▦ WEAK FILL LIGHT

Range of distances within which flashbulbs and electronic flash units can be used as main or fill light outdoors. The diagram is fully explained in the text on pages 72 and 74.

ble thickness gives about two stops reduction and so on.

In our diagrammatic survey the corresponding extended ranges are designated T 1 (single thickness), T 2 (double thickness), and T 3 (triple thickness). As an alternative the aperture can be closed down by one stop further. The daylight illuminated background will then of course be less well exposed, but this is not necessarily a drawback – on the contrary the result can often be pleasing.

The flash range under an overcast sky is considerably greater than in sunshine. This is as might be expected, for the flash naturally makes more impact in dull light than when in competition with direct sunlight.

When pictures are taken in the shade on a sunny day, the general light level is slightly higher than when the sky is overcast, and the flash range must accordingly be reduced by a quarter.

In our comparative survey the small electronic flash units show in general a pretty poor performance as compared with flashbulbs. This is particularly evident when we examine the range at $1/60$ sec. In fairness however I must admit that electronic flash has, when used with between-lens shutter cameras, the advantage that it can in any case be operated at $1/125$ sec. and in most cases even at $1/250$ and $1/500$ sec. (but this should be checked!). As every increase in shutter speed enables the stop to be opened further, this means an improvement in the flash range.

However there are limitations. Flashbulbs, even at shutter speeds of $1/30$ sec. and $1/60$ sec., permit long range shots with lens apertures of f4 or f4.5. Small electronic flash units (with 50ASA guide numbers of around 40 or 45) for comparable ranges demand apertures around f2 or a higher speed film. This in fact is a case where – exceptions prove the rule – film speed does play a part in the flash range. On the other hand with powerful electronic flash units and a shutter speed of $1/500$ sec. in dull weather even at 16 to 20 feet a subject can be brilliantly displayed against a deep black background.

Fill-in with automatic flash

Something far more than a mere note is called for on the technique of flash fill-in with automatic cameras (or to be more precise cameras with automatic exposure control), as well as daylight flash photography with cameras or flash equipment incorporating any form of automatic flash control.

Automatic cameras can as a rule be switched to "manual" operation or "flash", and can then be operated exactly in the same way as non-automatic equipment. In some cameras, switching over to the flash range couples the focusing mechanism to the stop control. This type of flash automation enables my $1/30$ sec. flash range data to be directly applied. It is however advisable to utilize only the front half of the permissible range; for if set to the longer distances the diaphragm will open very wide and the picture will be overexposed,

Automatic flash units using a sensor can also be used for outdoor photography, but with this type of equipment the stop must be individually set for every different film speed. A particular colour reversal film, used in conjunction with a particular computer flash unit, required a stop of from f4 to f5.6 However for relieving the shadows in sunshine f5.6 to f8 is needed if excessive fill-light is to be avoided.

Dealing with reflections

Just one really bright, penetrating reflection in a window, in polished furniture, or in a door can quite spoil the effect of a picture. In the case of a door or a casement window this can be avoided by opening the door or window just a little; the reflection will then take quite a different direction.

Unfortunately it is not every polished surface that can be thus easily moved. In such cases the best way might be to remove the flash unit from the camera and direct the flash on to the subject from one side. If this is not possible take two or three steps to one side so as to take a slightly oblique view of the subject, and with it the reflecting background. In this way it is possible to photograph through a shop window, a show case, or an aquarium (page 182) without incurring the slightest trouble from the reflections. All that is necessary is to ensure that the camera and its attached flash unit are viewing through the glass window with sufficient obliquity.

To ensure that any such reflections do not creep through to the finished picture unnoticed, particular care should be taken when shooting to see that no part of the subject appears unusually bright. Should it do so, repeat the shot after adjusting any suspected reflecting surfaces.

One thing which must be absolutely avoided is a reflection which can affect the automatic operation of a sensor flash unit or a sensor camera (Polaroid). The photoelectric cell responds to the bright reflection and, much too early, gives the order to the sensor unit to quench the flash (or to the sensor camera to close the shutter). In this way can arise underexposures which can be as severe as they are unexpected.

With flash on the camera a mirror must only be photographed obliquely from the side – sufficently obliquely to ensure that the flash is not reflected straight back into the camera lens.

Of course an "empty" mirror is not a very attractive subject: it needs something attractive reflected in it. This might be girl contemplating her reflection or maybe restoring her make-up. If you must fill the mirror with your own image, keep the camera – and flash – out of the picture.

The person thus photographed must of course be placed to the left of the mirror if the camera is to the right, and conversely to the right when the camera is on the left.

All this becomes obvious when you are taking the picture, but one thing that needs to be watched is the correct setting of the camera-subject distance. To focus on the mirror would be much too close. The correct setting is the total distance of camera to mirror plus mirror to subject. If the subject is at some distance from the mirror the latter will be completely out of focus. However this is of no importance: the main thing is that the reflected image is sharp. The actual surface of the mirror should be invisible anyway, whether sharp or unsharp. The mere fact that it is unsharp ensures that any scratches or fingerprints on its surface will become invisible – which is certainly no drawback!

Should any part of the mirror frame appear in the picture, it will of course be completely out of focus. But this, too, need not be regarded as a disadvantage. On the contrary, the greater the contrast between the sharp mirror image and the unsharp image of the mirror frame, the more interesting is the picture.

The total light path from the flash via the mirror to the model is just as important for the exposure as it is for focusing. The light shines on to the mirror and from there is reflected on to the face of the model. Her brightly illuminated face is reflected back by the mirror to form the image in the camera.

For an interesting portrait the model should not be lighted solely by dead frontal illumination: there should be a glint of light outlining the head. This characteristic back lighting feature is normally achieved by the use of a second lighting unit placed behind the model. In the case of a mirror picture, however, it can be provided by the one lamp on the camera. For this, two conditions must be fulfilled:

1 The camera must not view the mirror from too oblique an angle.
2 The camera must also be farther from the mirror than is the model.

Provided these conditions are fulfilled, it is possible with a single flash to obtain a mirror portrait with basically frontal lighting but with also a back lighting effect which would suggest the use of a second light source.

I have on occasion found this method very useful, as for instance when a young aspirant to the theatre handed me her camera with flash attached and with melting appeal begged me to make a really attractive picture of her. This meant using a mirror for the back lighting effect. The only other thing was to take care to reverse the negative back to front when enlarging.

Just one thing more: Only a fairly large mirror will ensure the success of this method. Glimpses of a face in a minute hand mirror are almost always spoilt by ugly shadow effects.

On the other hand it is not essential for the mirror, of whatever size, always to be included in the actual picture. Placed in the background behind a subject which is otherwise only frontally lighted, mirrors can be used to conjure up back or side lighting effects, or even, on occasion, small spots of light by reflecting the main light back on to the subject.

Care must of course be taken that the mirror itself is not visible in the viewfinder.

Effect of smoky atmosphere

To take a flash picture in a smoke filled area without special precautions is – at least so far as colour is concerned – just waste of time.

Not long ago Kodak made a series of tests on colour material in an average living room measuring 4.25 × 4.25 × 2.80 metres (14 × 14 × 9.2 ft). After the 12th cigarette had made its smoke contribution, pictures were coming out rather flat. For good measure they also exhibited a sourish yellow cast. An astonishing thing however was that even after one solitary cigarette had been smoked in the room the photographs showed unmistakable colour cast and loss of brilliance.

There is in fact nothing remarkable about this. The light has to pass twice through the smoke screen. On their first journey, from flash to subject, many of the rays are scattered and reflected back by the minute smoke particles. The remaining light which succeeds in reaching and illuminating the subject, is still further weakened on its return journey back to the camera, and its fall-out, as on the outward journey, results in light scatter which forms a kind of luminous yellow curtain screening the subject.

The problem is very similar to that of underwater photography, wherein so many flash shots are obscured by light scatter from floating particles. In that case the danger can be largely obviated by restricting photography to close-ups.

The best precaution to take against the yellow cast resulting from this blue haze is to open the window, let the fresh air in, and stop smoking! Smoke is not perhaps so deadly to black-and-white film as to colour material, but the resulting negatives come out very flat. This however is relatively easy to compensate by using harder material, and so far as that goes merely by using a yellow, or better still an orange filter when making the exposure. A really drastic precaution is to use a red filter or even infra-red material.

Handkerchiefs and the background

What has a handkerchief to do with the background? More than at first sight might appear. If when taking a flash shot indoors a corner of a handkerchief is held in front of the flash reflector the flash will be dimmed. This will call for a larger stop, and it necessarily follows that the background will be thrown further out of focus.

This unsharpness, however, is just what is needed. It has already been emphasized that two phenomena in particular are responsible for typical faults which frequently mar frontal flash photographs:

1 The "sticking" of the subject to the background.
2 The black outlining shadow.

The unsharpness of the background resulting from the wider aperture both preveents the "sticking" effect and also softens into pleasing insignificance the shadows which otherwise would mar the background.

Needless to say, the background must be separated by at least some distance from the subject, otherwise increasing the aperture cannot make any difference to its sharpness.

How much the aperture must in fact be increased to compensate for the diffusion introduced by the handkerchief depends on the opacity of the material. As a rough guide the aperture may be opened one stop for each thickness of the handkerchief.

So far we have been concerned only with the reduction in illumination intensity resulting from the interposition of a diffusing screen in front of the reflector. Nothing has been said of how and why this device "softens" the illumination of the subject, and why in fact it does "soften" the shadows. This is an effect the value of which has frequently been described in the most glowing terms, but which in fact is far less frequently so successful in practice.

The fact that "softened" flash under particular circumstances perhaps, with certain assumptions and reservations, and many "ifs" and "buts" occasionally does "soften" the illumination can be attributed to two quite different causes: the one concerns the size of the illuminated surface by which the subject is lighted. In the flash gun of today this surface is as a rule very small. If a handkerchief, a serviette, or a sheet of translucent paper is held in front of such a flash gun, the effective spot of light which is formed upon it is only very slightly larger than the reflector. This is a vitally important factor, for if the spot is to be so greatly increased in size that it has a substantial effect on the shadow structure (pages   et seq) and therefore on the subject contrast, the diffusing screen must be moved out some distance from the reflector. In the case of a camera with built-in flash, this would scarcely be possible without the screen encroaching upon the field of view of the lens or at least introducing objectionable scattered light.

The shadow-relieving soft lighting effect produced in this way is most successful in close-ups and macrophotographs. Here there is already a degree of softening present consequent upon the very short working distance, the built-in flash itself introducing a certain amount of side light. Large soft shadows result, with very attractive effect.

The other reason why a softening effect on the lighting is claimed for the diffusing screen technique lies in the fact that it somewhat broadens the coverage of the flash. In particular it relaxes a little the close concentration of the electronic flash within the subject area. This has the effect of spreading some of the light over reflecting surfaces on the walls and ceiling of the room, thereby improving the general indirect lighting. This effect however is really only worth considering when the room decor is very light in tone and the flash-subject distance is considerable – in short when the indirect lighting is good anyway. So far as unembellished frontal flash is concerned there is nothing that needs such fill lighting except the accompanying cast shadow outlining the subject.

Varying the lighting effect with wide angle and telephoto lenses

Unbelievable as it may sound, it is nevertheless true: frontal flash lighting gives different results – and not only in the matter of exposure – with a wide angle lens from those obtained with the normal lens. And a telephoto lens gives a different effect again.

Let us be clear about this: If the camera is set up in a fixed position, and only the lens is changed, then nothing will happen to the lighting: changing the lens will only alter the amount of the subject which appears on the film. But if the object is to photo-

Effects of diffusion. A, At a small stop, depth of field is great. B, With flash diffused, a larger aperture is required. Depth of field is reduced and background becomes less obtrusive. C, Direct flash throws harsh shadow. D, Diffused flash has slight softening effect.

graph always on the same scale, using a short focus lens from close up, a normal focus lens from a more distant viewpoint, and a long focus lens from a still greater distance, the lighting effects will be very different in the three cases: With the short focus lens the background will appear dark; the normal focus lens will give "medium" background illumination; with the long focus the background will appear quite well lighted.

In all three cases, be it clearly understood, the flash exposure is calculated for the foreground subject, which therefore is equally exposed in each case. Likewise the subject-background distance remains the same throughout and the flash is in each case on the camera. The varying background illumination is thus caused by the increased ratio of flash-to-subject and subject-to-background distance. The greater this ratio the less the fall-off in illumination behind the subject – and, incidentally, the less the increase in illumination in front of the subject.

This leads to another interesting possibility. Let us suppose we are stalking a cat which is playing a lively game with a ball of wool. It jumps hither and thither, backward and forward, continually altering its distance from the camera – and therefore from the flash. To attempt to snap it with the wide angle lens from close up would mean following it with the camera forward or backward with practically every jump, or – a practical impossibility – continually readjusting the stop. With the steep fall off in light intensity with distance, there will be a great probability that some pictures will be over, and others underexposed.

If on the other hand we use a longer focus lens and operate from a greater distance, the cat would have to jump considerable distances to make any serious difference to the intensity of the light falling upon it. The operator is thus left to concentrate upon keeping the cat in focus without bothering about the stop.

Indirect or "bounce" flash

To attempt to bring bounce flash under the heading of "frontal" lighting is somewhat stretching the point, because often enough one or more accessories are needed which are normally used for independent flash techniques (see page 90).

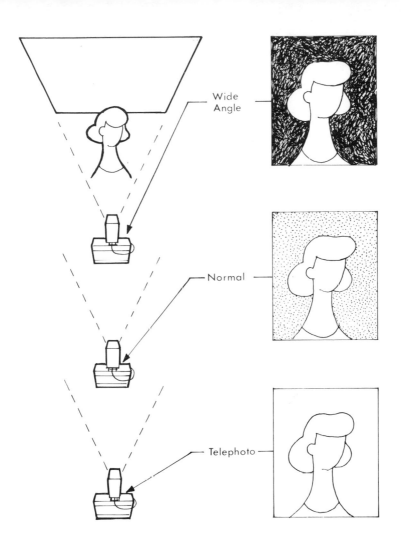

Wide Angle

Normal

Telephoto

Effect of shooting distance. With flash on camera and lenses and viewpoint changed to maintain image size, background illumination varies with shooting distance. At long range, the background is almost as well illuminated as the subject.

For bounce flash, the flash unit is still attached to the camera, but its light is directed upward (see page 85). Thus the light does not, as with normal flash, illuminate the subject directly, but only by reflection from the ceiling. This reflected light – always provided the ceiling is light in tone – then gives a widely scattered illumination over the whole scene.

The most important characteristics of bounce lighting can be summed up as follows:

1 The subject is softly lighted, i. e. free from harsh cast shadows, and of course there is no "outlining" cast shadow on the background. This is an advantage in flash photography, because one can be quite certain that there will nowhere be ugly shadows which could ruin the picture. The lighting is quite soft and uniform, closely resembling natural lighting under a clouded sky. This is a most satisfactory type of lighting for portraits, group snapshots and so forth.

2 With bounce lighting the entire room is completely uniformly lighted – the background equally with the main subject. The resulting pictures never have the appearance so often referred to as "typical flash pictures".

3 A great deal of light is lost in indirect flash. However even this can have its advantages. The lower general lighting level demands a wider aperture, which automatically puts the background out of focus. There is thus a sharpness contrast between foreground and background.

4 The uniform lighting throughout the room is of inestimable advantage for snapshot work. Anything anywhere in the room, at any distance from the camera – and therefore from the flash – can be shot without a thought to the exposure, and without at any time altering the "standard" stop. So long as we continue to use bounce flash, any simple flash gun becomes elevated to the status of an automatic unit.

5 Because a large stop is used, the general room lighting, of whatever kind, is much better able to compete with the flash. The room lights are much better recorded than with frontal flash and are able to make their own contribution to the general atmosphere.

6 There are scarcely any obtrusive reflections in bounce flash

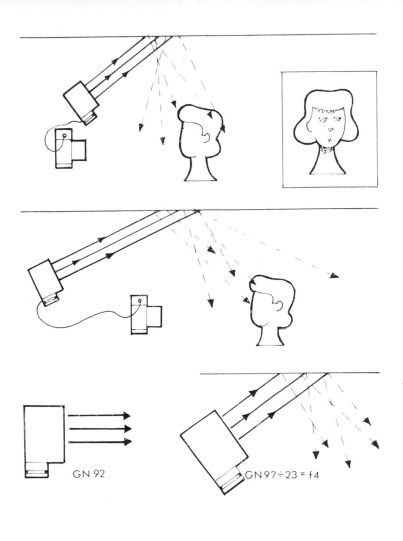

GN 92

GN 92 ÷ 23 = f4

Bounced flash. If the angle is too steep, shadows appear under nose, chin and in eye-sockets. At a less steep angle the light is softer and is thrown over a broader area. A rule of thumb for exposure adjustment in medium-sized rooms is to divide the guide number by 23.

pictures. Window panes, spectacle lenses, polished furniture no longer throw harsh reflections back into the camera: any reflections they do give are quite unobtrusive. For the same reason, bounce flash lends itself very well to the photography of silverware, bronze plaques, and other objet d'art exhibiting polished surfaces.

One important point must be emphasized. The bounced light should not be directed too steeply upward so as to produce a bright, but comparatively small circle of light directly above the subject. This acts as top lighting, which is not very satisfactory. Moreover such lighting can quite easily produce cast shadows at various points – for example the eye sockets – which, while not exactly black, are sufficiently obvious to be objectionable. It also tends to emphasize wrinkles and creases. By directing the light obliquely upwards a much more pleasant lighting is obtained, and this is the only way to get really soft shadows in the pictures. While bounce lighting completely does away with deep black shadows, it does produce a light, scarcely noticeable shadow effect. It is due to this that subjects photographed by indirect lighting exhibit a far greater impression of relief than is possible with direct frontal flash. Unfortunately the oblique illumination of the ceiling necessitates that the flash-subject distance should not be too short, because otherwise no other course remains but to direct the flash steeply upwards. If this were not done, the greater part of the light reflected from the ceiling would miss the subject and fall on the background.

If the worst comes to the worst, the only way out is to use an extension cable to enable the flash to be placed well behind the camera – maybe on a tripod (see page 96).

It has already been pointed out that bounce flash uses a lot of light. But just how much? There are many answers to this question, some of them with some foundation, some pure conjecture. We propose to ignore all such advice and recount only our own experience on the subject.

So far as medium size rooms with medium-toned decorations are concerned, divide the guide number of the flash gun by 23, or look up in a table the stop corresponding to 23 feet working distance. Set the camera lens to this stop.

For use with bounce flash, electronic flash is not quite so good as flash bulbs. Its cone of light is much less widely spread, because the reflectors used are relatively small and in consequence the area of walls and ceiling which they illuminate is smaller. To cut a long story short, electronic flash calls for a larger stop.

In rooms which are smaller and lighter in tone than an average living room, less light is lost. The whole exposure situation is analysed briefly, but it is hoped concisely, in the following table:

EXPOSURE RECOMMENDATIONS FOR BOUNCED FLASH

| Room | Stop for bounce flash | |
	Flash bulbs	Electronic flash
Normal size, average light toned rooms (living rooms)	Divide guide number by 23	Divide guide number by 40
Small, extremely light toned rooms (bathrooms, modern kitchens)	Divide guide number by 16	Divide guide number by 26 to 30
Very large rooms with white ceiling (halls)	Divide guide number by light path (flash-ceiling-subject) and open up one further stop	Divide guide number by light path (flash-ceiling-subject) and open up $2^{1}/_{2}$ further stops

The above data relate to reversal films. Black-and-white films are not quite so demanding. Quite satisfactory results can be obtained with apertures one stop smaller.

Computer flash equipment should in general be set to manual operation for indirect lighting. Those units with stop selection provision, however, are suitable for use automatically. In these, the sensor is still directed toward the subject when the tilting reflector head is directed upward. Thus the automatic function operates both with indirect and semi-indirect lighting.

Even where colour reversal films are used, however, there is no need for concern that the above rough guide may on occasion fail. Exposure with bounce flash is not all that critical. After all, underexposure – with reversal film – just means that the shadows will be blocked up, i. e. completely black. Overexposure means that the highlights will be burned out, making these areas as transparent as glass. Now where the lighting contrast is very high, so that both highlights and shadows come near to the limit of acceptability, the slightest over- or underexposure will endanger the whole transparency.

However with very few exceptions bounce flash photographs are always extremely soft and uniform in their lighting. It would be necessary to overexpose very considerably before detail became lost in even a relatively light toned area and to greatly underexpose before shadow detail became impenetrably back.

For use with indirect flash it is in any case essential to be able to open up the aperture to at least f5.6 or better still to f4.5. It is useless to attempt bounce flash photography with very simple cameras, the more so as it is usually a difficult matter to use ultra speed films or gigantic screw cap flash bulbs with them.

So far, nothing has been said as to how, in any case, the upward tilt of the flash is achieved.

Where the flash unit is connected to the camera with a synchronizing cable this presents no difficulty. A flash tilting attachment in the accessory shoe of the camera or on the flash bracket enables the flash to be tilted upwards in any direction. Cameras with centre contact flash equipment require the addition at least of an accessory such as is described on page 91. Bounce flash is in fact a sort of hybrid – not exactly *on* the camera, not exactly independent.

There is one accessory which enables the light from any flash source – even when built into the camera – to be directed upwards. A small hand mirror. Provided the light output is sufficient, it can even be held in front of a flash cube to give bounce lighting.

Flash
off the
Camera

When the flash unit is built into the camera, you have no option but to use frontal lighting for nearly all your flash shots. Most subjects, however, can be more pleasantly rendered by placing the flash to one side of the camera and perhaps above the normal eye level. As the synchronising leads provided with flash units are generally quite short, an essential item of equipment is an extension flash cable with standard coaxial connectors. If the camera has only a "hot shoe" type contact an adaptor must be obtained to convert it to a flash socket type.

Accessories for particular purposes

Flash tilt attachment: For indirect flash. Slips into the accessory shoe on the camera or the flash bracket, and enables the flash to be directed upwards at any angle.

Flash unit attachment shoes: An adapter with an accessory shoe into which the flash unit can be slid. Underneath is a tripod screw socket accepting either british or Continental tripod screws. (The adaptation of one screw thread to the other is effected by an intermediate screw or conversion screw). This accessory will convert any ball and socket tripod head into a flash tilting device, and any camera tripod into a practical flash gun holder.

Clampod: Used in conjunction with an accessory shoe forms an ideal holder for flashbulb or electronic flash units for fixing to chair backs, mantelpieces, branches of trees, etc.

Spiral cables: These so-called "coiled cords" are extension cables of 5–6 feet in length. They automatically close down to a tight helix only an inch or two long.

Lens hoods: For excluding internal reflections especially from side and backlighting.

Test Lamps: Available with capless base, AG cap and flash cube fitting. Assists detection of faulty contacts in the flash circuit.

About extension cables

Once we decide to separate the flash from the camera we have naturally to abandon the usual close connection between them.

EXTENSION CABLES AND ADAPTORS

Type of camera	Type of flash unit	Accessory equipment
Cameras with flash socket for extension cable	Units with synchro-nizing lead, or com-bined type for alter-native accessory shoe centre contact, or flash cube units with synchronizing lead	Standard extension cable
Cameras with flash socket for extension cable	Units with centre contact only, or corresponding flash cube units	Standard extension cable plus adapter centre contact (on unit) to standard flash socket (on camera) or: 5 metre cable drum with standard coaxial plug and centre contact shoe on upper side of drum
Cameras with accessory shoe centre contact only	Units with synchro-nizing lead, or com-bined type for alter-native accessory shoe centre contact, or flash cube units with synchronizing lead	Standard extension cable plus adapter from centre contact (on camera) to co-axial plug (on exten-sion lead from flash unit)
Cameras with accessory shoe centre contact only	Units with centre contact only, or corresponding flash cube units	5 metre cable drum with standard plug and centre contact acessory shoe on upper side plus shoe adapter or: Standard extension cable, plus shoe adapter plus cable adapter

The connection must be still maintained because the triggering "switch" for the flash is in the camera shutter. For the lengthened connection between camera and flash we need an extension cable. This may be anything between 20 inches and some 30 feet in length. A good length for general use is between 5 feet and 7 feet. Too long an extension cable can lead to disasters. This happened to a photographer once – during a ball! He was trying to get a particularly tender and artistically lighted picture of Mireille Matthieu. Camera to eye, flash high at arms's length, he made a dive for her – and fell at her feet! He had caught his feet in the trip wire entanglement of his overlong cable. Needless to say, this brought the house down: everybody laughed their heads off – except the photographer!

Nevertheless one cannot continue indefinitely to harbour resentment against 15 feet of cable; for some – indeed for many lighting problems it is indispensable. And if you can have available one cable each of 5, 10 and 15 feet length you should be equipped for every conceivable flash situation. If need be, all three cables can be connected together, giving a total length of 30 feet.

In the far distant past it was an accepted fact that flash can only be operated with complete certainty up to a cable length of 16 feet. My own experience is that cables up to 100 feet in length can be used with complete success. Electronic flash and flash bulbs both function perfectly. Admittedly for flash bulb equipment I use powerful capacitor flash units with 15 or 22.5 volt batteries. In order to reduce to an absolute minimum any contact resistance in the flashbulb mount I place the cap of the flashbulb in my mouth before inserting it in the holder.

Naturally the battery should be in reasonably good condition; these batteries can remain usable for up to three years, or even longer. This has the drawback that one tends to forget all about them, and in the meantime they run right out.

This once happened to me – quite suddenly – at a really crucial photographic occasion. The battery just completely died on me. I warmed it carefully over a candle flame, and this sufficed to meet the most pressing needs of the occasion. Since then I have made a point of changing the batteries every time I change my shirt – that is, at least every Christmas!

However it is not fair always to blame a flash failure on the battery.

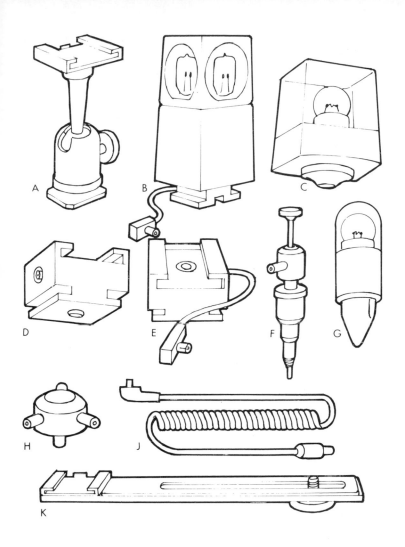

Equipment and accessories. A, Bounce flash attachment. B, Flash-cube. C, Test bulb. D, Adapter for connecting flash cable to accessory shoe contacts. E, Adaptor for converting camera contacts to accessory shoe contacts. F, Mechanical synchroniser. G, Test bulb. H, Multiple connection plug. J, Extension cable. K, Flash bracket.

93

More often than not it is not the cause. As a rule it will be found that connections have not been properly plugged in, or have subsequently come loose. In a well worn cable the conductor may have actually become severed. In most cases this happens just beneath the plug or socket.

In the event of a failure I first check the flash unit without using the cable (in the case of flash bulb equipment using, of course, a test lamp). Then I put in circuit one length of cable after another, checking in each case that the unit is functioning. This procedure is continued until a failure occurs. Then I know that the last length of cable is responsible.

Supporting the flash

A favourite method of using independent flash is to hold the flashgun in the hand, and this works quite well so long as the old snapshot rule is adhered to, whereby the lens stop and focus are simply set once and for all, and left untouched throughout a whole series of exposures. Admittedly, it requires a little practice to keep the flash accurately trained on the subject with the left hand, while the right hand holds and operates the camera. Sometimes a self-timer is of assistance here.

Unfortunately it is not in every case that sufficient side light effect is obtainable by merely holding the flashgun with arm outstretched. Years ago I photographed a sculpture in a castle in this way from a distance of 40 feet. In the resulting photograph there was no detectable difference in the frontal lighting effect. The only noticeable difference lay in the outlining shadows in the background, which had become broader and more obtrusive than they would otherwise have been. The lighting effect is in fact dependent not only upon how far the light source is moved to the side of the camera, but also upon the distance of the subject. In extreme close-ups and macrophotography, for instance, the side lighting becomes evident even when the flash is mounted on a bracket attached to the camera. To ensure that the subject receives the full flood of the lighting, the flash unit is in this case merely turned slightly in its direction.

At a distance of 20 inches, even a glancing light effect can be

Flash off camera. With extension cables and two flashguns you can provide more attractive lighting schemes. A long extension cable to a remote flash is a useful set-up for photographing young children.

achieved by holding the flashgun in the outstretched hand (page 94). If the subject distance is further increased, only a side lighting effect is obtainable, and from a distance of 6 feet upwards there is next to no difference as compared with strictly frontal lighting. Only by lengthening the flash cable and stretching the arm to the limit will it perhaps be found possible to conjure up some degree of side lighting effect at, say, 10 feet.

For a number of reasons there is frequently no choice but to move the flash unit a good deal further sideways than the arm could possibly reach. This is where the longer extension cable comes in. Where previously a 3-foot lead sufficed we now need 10 or even 15 feet. With such freedom of movement it becomes possible to light the subject from any angle – not only from the front, but also from the side or even from behind.

It is a great help if the flashgun can be given to someone else to hold. In point of fact, holding a flash unit is no child's play! It is only too easy so to direct it that the bulk of the light just misses the subject, and it does actually call for the greatest care to ensure that it is accurately aimed. With electronic flash, whose beam is more concentrated, it is much easier to miss the target than with the wider spread flash bulb illumination.

Should you be of the diffident type, and do not care to ask a bystander to act for a few moments as lighting assistant, you will need to look for some other support for the flash unit: it can for instance be tied to the back of a chair or secured in the fork of a tree branch. One makeshift method is to wedge it between two piles of books. Of course, you can always slip it on a tripod.

To mount a flashgun on a tripod, an adapter is needed having an accessory shoe for the flashgun and a screw socket for the tripod screw. Strangely enough only a very few flashguns are supplied fitted with a tripod socket. As to the type of tripod, I confess my own preference is for the clampod! It enables the flash gun to be fixed to the edge of a door, to a picture frame, the back of a chair, a Christmas tree, a floor vase, or even a pair of antlers.

As an example of this I recently had occasion to photograph some children playing in a room. The flashgun I had secured to the edge of a book shelf, but I used the camera in the hand. A 10-foot cable enabled me to take snapshots from the most varied positions, and under the widest possible lighting conditions.

The result was a harmonious blend, in one film, of side and back lightings, frontal and glancing light. There were general views, and close-ups of faces and hands, snapped from above, one after another, higgledy piggledy.

Exposure for flash

The exposure for a reversal film with side, glancing, or back lighting – or for that matter with any kind of lighting with independent flash – differs only insignificantly from that of frontal flash. Here, as there, it is best to start from the guide number or stop table. Here I am quite prepared for some lively protests. For it is fairly generally maintained that the diaphragm must be opened up by $1/2$ stop when the light falls on the subject from an angle of about 45° (the angle made by the lighting axis with the camera axis). A 90° angle calls for one stop increase in aperture, back lighting for as much as two stops.

Granted, under certain conditions (see page 99) such increases in aperture are indeed advisable – especially with negative film. The above recommendation cannot therefore be unreservedly recommended – in particular not for every film. However let us for the moment consider only reversal film. Here overexposure is admissible for one special case – namely copying (page 189). In point of fact a large photograph or painting, if lighted from about 45°, demands the sacrifice of $1/2$ stop. If for any reason it should be desired to use an 80° glancing illumination, it would cost a whole stop.

But how often do we in fact have to photograph a subject as flat as this? Perhaps 1 in 10 000 subjects: the rest are of a spatial character.

Things are then very different. Take for instance the most perfect of all spatial objects – the sphere.

One such is our friend the moon. As viewed from the earth at the quarter, the sun lights it obliquely from one side, so that we can only see one side of it. The part facing the sun – to be precise the centre of the hemisphere facing it – is illuminated just as brightly as, at full moon, the whole of the moon's surface facing us.

Thus while it is true that glancing light illuminates only a fraction of the whole area presented to us by the subject – in the case of the moon only a half – on the other hand within this illuminated area there are always to be found features which reflect the light toward the camera with special intensity, just as does the "skin" of a frontally lighted subject (sometimes even more intensely). In consequence, side lighting or glancing illumination does not call for a larger stop than does frontal lighting: a larger stop would involve a risk of overexposure of the most brightly illuminated features, with resulting burning out. The intensity of the projection light will ensure that detail is squeezed out of even the blackest area of a transparency.

If however it is desired to lighten the darkest shadows, we can always resort to some kind of fill-light (reflecting screen, tele light). Overexposure is not to be recommended! More precisely, while overexposure may be permissible, it rather depends upon the subject. Personally, as I have said, I am not in favour of lightening dark subjects by overexposure and conversely. On the other hand there is no closing one's eyes to the fact that the intrinsic tone of the subject, particularly when the lighting contrast is high, has a decided influence on exposure latitude. A light yellow sphere illuminated by glancing light will bleach out on the side towards the light with relatively slight over-exposure, all detail being completely lost.

A deep red sphere, on the other hand, may be overexposed up to perhaps two stops, with consequent advantage to shadow detail. Certainly on the extreme edge the colour will tend to light red, but all the detail will still be there. With reversal film the exposure must be determined by the brightest features of the subject.

The reverse is the case with negative film, where exposure is governed by the darkest features of the subject. Frontal lighting produces practically no shadows. As soon as the flash is allowed to introduce a side component to the lighting, shadows at one begin to appear, and more extensive areas of the subject remain darker than is the case with frontal lighting. The exposure therefore has to be increased, as circumstances dictate, by the equivalent of one, or maybe even two stops.

So far, only side lighting and glancing light have been discussed. Top lighting and footlights, however, call for the same treatment: they come into the same category as side lighting.

Exposure for back lighting with flash

Here the area of the subject actually facing the camera receives far less light than under glancing, not to mention frontal lighting. But again there is a proviso: overexposure would be basically necessary if all subjects scattered light ideally on reflection. This is in fact practically never the case. Almost always the reflection is a combination of scattered and concentrated (specularly reflected) light.

In particular, even the most pronouncedly matt surface suddenly assumes specular reflecting properties with backlighting. This is well illustrated by the case of a girl in a black pullover. Under frontal lighting the pullover appears uniformly black and featureless. Only backlighting is able to conjure up around even the blackest black a relatively light grey rim of light showing up every least unevenness. This rim comprises in fact nothing other than the reflection of the glancing illumination, which by its nature is relatively highly concentrated.

I have tested out the most unlikely subjects with glancing backlighting: hexagonal cardboard prisms, oranges, eggs, heads and balls of wall. The brightness of the light reflected in the direction of the camera was investigated with sensitive measuring equipment as well as by trial exposures.

My general conclusion after all these experiments is that in most cases the brightest part of the subject is concentrated in a narrow rim outlining the subject. This rim, however, is as a rule so bright that its intrinsic brilliance is even higher than that of surfaces illuminated from the same distance by frontal lighting. So, for negative film in backlighting the same general flash rules apply as for side and glancing light. The aperture should be opened up a further one or two stops. Reversal films on the other hand need one stop smaller aperture, especially, of course, when the subject is partly translucent.

Direction of lighting and its effect

Before dealing in detail with all the potentialities in practice of fill-in flash lighting it is important to define precisely what is meant by the various types of lighting – back lighting, glancing light, side lighting and so forth.

Every different direction of lighting – by which of course is meant the deviation of the direction of the illuminating light from direct aiming of the illumination from camera position to subject – produces an *effect* peculiar to itself, maybe even a number of effects. Basically, any particular direction of lighting can produce two quite different – sometimes completely opposite – effects. In the one case there is the pure lighting effect unrelieved by any fill-light, with full lighting contrast: in the other, exactly the same lighting modified by an added fill light.

I am almost tempted to say that the difference in effect between, say, glancing light on the one hand and under, or low-angle, lighting on the other is still not as great as that between glancing or low angle light with and without fill light.

The great prototype for every photographic light source – the sun – to all appearances circles the earth. Taking this as a model, let us suppose our flash gun in similar fashion to circle around the subject.

The camera – at first, at any rate – must be supposed to occupy a fixed position. Close beside it is the flashgun. Its first orbit is a horizontal one around the subject. So long as it remains close to the camera it gives frontal lighting; this changes gradually to side lighting, then to rim lighting. Passing through the rim lighting zone it finally arrives at the back lighting position. From there it returns, on the other side of the subject, through rim lighting, side lighting, back to frontal lighting beside the camera.

We can instead choose a vertical orbit, so to speak from pole to pole. From frontal lighting it passes through high angle lighting, top lighting, top rim lighting, to back lighting. The other half of the orbit lies for the most part in an area where it is impossible to set up the flash – unless the subject is not resting on the ground but supported somehow in mid air. Following this comes the low-angle front lighting zone, and finally frontal lighting from beside the camera.

All the designations relating to the vertical lighting orbit can of course apply only to a subject situated in front of the camera, so that "above" and "below" have their normal significance. For pictures taken from a precarious vantage point on a chandelier,

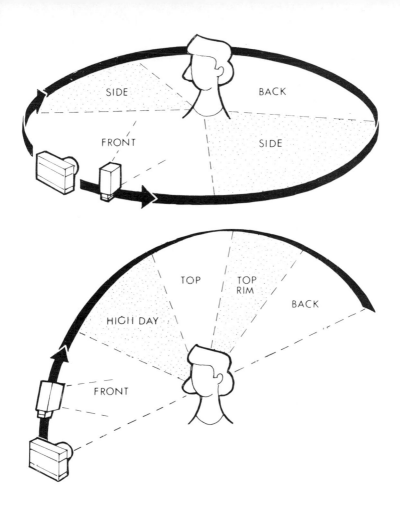

The lighting effect varies as the flash is moved around the subject, horizontally or vertically. For these effects, of course, the camera remains in the same position and the flash is moved independently.

101

looking from above into an aquarium, there can be no top or underlighting, but only side lighting.

For the rest, we do in fact scarcely ever use a flashgun in a position strictly on either a vertical or a horizontal orbit. In ninety-nine cases out of a hundred we have to do with intermediate positions such as high side lighting or side top lighting, both of which mean the same and come under the general heading of cross lighting. An analysis of lighting directions and the effects they produce is given in the following table:

DIRECTION OF LIGHTING AND ITS EFFECT

Type of lighting	Angle between camera axis and lighting axis	Effect in portraiture	Effect in product photography	Applications
Front, or frontal lighting, flat lighting	From 0 to at most 20 to either side or up or down. The flash thus illuminates the subject more or less along the camera axis.	Portraits show lack of modelling; hence the expression `flat` lighting. Objectionable outlining cast shadows on background if this is close and light in tone. Face appears rather broad, but wrinkles and skin blemishes are largely suppressed	Lack of modelling and general surface characteristics. Unsuitable for product photography.	Flash snapshots with frontal lighting. Can often improve lighting quality when used as auxiliary fill-light.
Side lighting	From 20 to at most 80 preferably in a horizontal direction.	Side lighting with auxiliary fill-light is the standard lighting for portraiture. Modelling of facial characteristics is emphasized	Emphasizes three-dimensional characteristics of the subject	A high side lighting may be regarded as one type of standard lighting. For further details see page 103
Rim lighting	From at least 80 to at most 100 preferably in a horizontal plane. The lighting axis is approximately at right angles to the camera axis.	Strong lighting contrast giving pronounced light and shade effects. Emphasizes modelling, but only when assisted by fill-light.	Emphasizes surface structure.	Further details on page 104

Type of Lighting	Angle between camera axis and lighting axis	Effect in portraiture	Effect in product photography	Applications
Top lighting	From at least 20 to at most 80 vertical eleva-tion.	As standard lighting for por-traiture a cross lighting between side and top lighting is to be preferred.		Further details below
Top rim lighting	From at least 80 to 100 in the vertical plane through the camera axis.	As with side rim lighting. In por-traiture. suitable only as auxiliary lighting.	Glancing light effect.	Used mostly only as auxiliary lighting.
Low angle or under lighting. lighting from below. foot-lighting	20 or more ver-tically below camera level.	Special effects. dramatic. cari-cature and horror portraits.	Occasionally used to produce heavy cast sha-dows of the sub-ject on the ground.	Further details on page 104
Back lighting. fringe lighting	More than 100 from the camera axis. irrespective of direction. the light source shines more or less back along the camera axis. Since. however. it is hidden be-hind the subject. the result is extreme back lighting.	A mysterious fringe of light forms around the subject, and this effect can be utilized to sep-arate a subject from a back-ground of similar hue. At night it shows up the out-line of a dark subject against a black background.	Translucent ob-jects glass. flowers assume a mysterious glow.	A very effective lighting which is most valuable with or without fill-lighting Further details on page 130

As already mentioned, top lighting, directed from one side, can be effectively used as standard lighting for portraiture and group photography. However so far as possible the light should be di-rected on the side of the face (at $^1/_4$, $^1/_2$, $^3/_4$ or full profile) which is turned somewhat away from the camera. If the opposite course is followed, and the flash is shone full on the larger half of the face it will appear – not always, but nearly always – as if the sitter were suffering from mumps.

For a deep group, the light should be placed as high as possible. The higher it is, the more even will be the illumination throughout the depth of the room.

The reason for this is of course that the steep angle of the lighting limits the difference between the two light paths – from flash to foreground and flash to background.

Once in Arcadia I had to light a small square perfectly evenly at night. A festival was in progress. People sat eating roast mutton and drinking bright red wine. In the background was heard the sound of the bousoukis. I took a flash shot from the second floor of my small hotel. I had fixed the flashgun as high as I possibly could on the window frame, aiming it straight at the farthermost corner of the square. Thus the centre of the beam, which is always the most intense, illuminated the people who were in fact quite a long way away. The foreground on the other hand received light only from the edge of the beam. This simple trick enabled me to get perfectly uniform lighting from front to back.

Underlighting is the opposite of top lighting, and equally the opposite of all normal lighting set-ups. Its effect is to transform a normal expression into an ugly grimace – to give it a demonic, sinister character. On the other hand, relieved with a little fill-lighting, underlighting can lend a touch of sex appeal to a pretty girl, and make her appear really attractive. The strangeness of the atmosphere introduced by underlighting may be explained by the fact that it is hardly ever met with in nature, except perhaps in features lit from below by firelight, Chinese lanterns, or candles. Such lighting can be impressively simulated by under-lighting of the type described.

In hard *rim lighting,* shapes lose their accustomed relationships. Unrelated bright spots appear out of the darkness – torn fragments of a disintegrated subject. This is not necessarily without interest, and in particular it can contribute to an atmosphere partaking of the uncanny, the inexplicable, the incomprehensible. However, provided adequate fill-lighting is present to relieve the dense shadows, the subject stands suddenly revealed in a quite remarkable clarity of detail: in particular the modelling appears accentuated, even extraordinarily accentuated. The charm of the three-dimensional – of bas-reliefs, and wood and stone sculpture – is much enhanced.

At this point it would seem appropriate to turn to a discussion of the various methods of providing fill-lighting, and the following sections are therefore devoted to this subject.

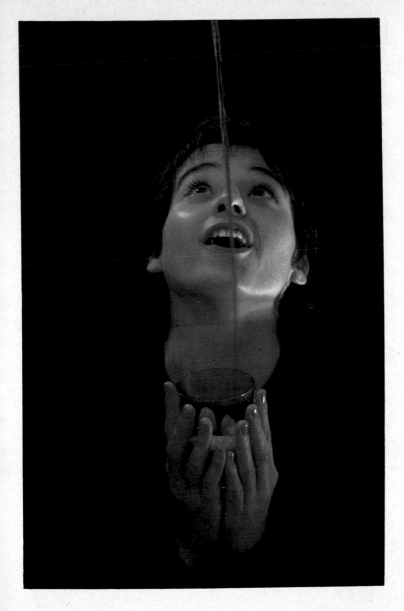

The raining red wine is lit by one flash from the side and a little backward. Two other lamps shine on a white wall behind the camera to provide a strong frontal fill lighting.

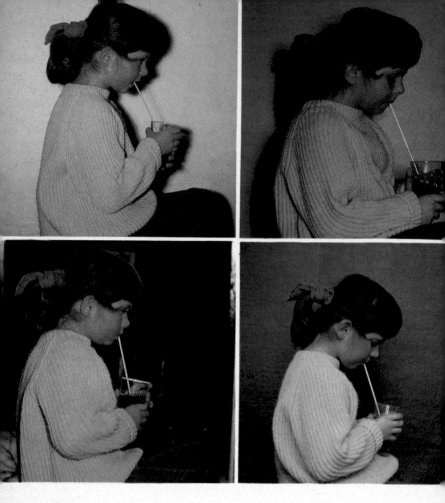

Except for the final picture on the opposite page all the pictures on these two pages were taken with a single flash. At top left, the flash was near the camera with the inevitable background shadow close to the figure. An improvement was obtained in the next picture by raising the camera and directing the flash slightly from the right. The shadow then falls lower down behind the head and back and is not so distracting. At bottom left the shadow disappears altogether when the model is placed before an open door or window. The right-hand picture was taken by indirect light, the flash being bounced off a large white reflector.

The top two pictures are typical silhouettes. The light is behind the model in each case and is directed at a yellow wall. The left-hand picture received three stops less exposure than that on the right so that less detail appeared in the figure to give a more genuine silhouette effect. The bottom two pictures are against-the-light shots. The lights were turned round and shone on the model instead of on the wall. No additional light was used for the left-hand picture but the other has achieved detail in the figure from the use of a weak frontal fill-in light. These eight pictures illustrate the varied effects that can be obtained with simple equipment.

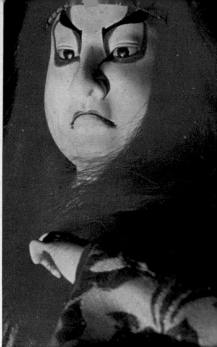

Three photographs of a Japanese lion-dancer doll using just one flash unit. *Above left:* The flash was near to the camera but in a raised position slightly to the left. *Left:* Side-top lighting directed at the side of the face farthest from the camera. *Above:* Underlighting by directing the flash steeply upward from below and slightly to the left.

Opposite: A ½-sec exposure enabled a sharp flash image to be superimposed on the unsharp reddish image produced by the stage lighting.

Page 110: A large blue flashbulb and daylight illuminated this impressive dome for a shot on daylight film.

Page 111: A moderately long focus lens and a giant blue flashbulb placed on the floor within the arch captured this shot of a Byzantine mosaic.

The drummer's hands are lit from one side with a blue flashbulb. The close approach concentrates all attention on the hands.

Stage shot of an actor from the folk-lore show "Brasiliana". Lighting was with a blue flashbulb on daylight film.

Above: A honey bee at a cowslip photographed at life size. A single electronic flash was mounted on a bracket attached to the camera. At such close range it provided effective side lighting.
Opposite: The same set-up was used to photograph this brimstone butterfly alighting on a thistle.

A glancing side light from the left illuminates the stamens of a hibiscus blossom. A second flash was used to light the translucent petals from behind.

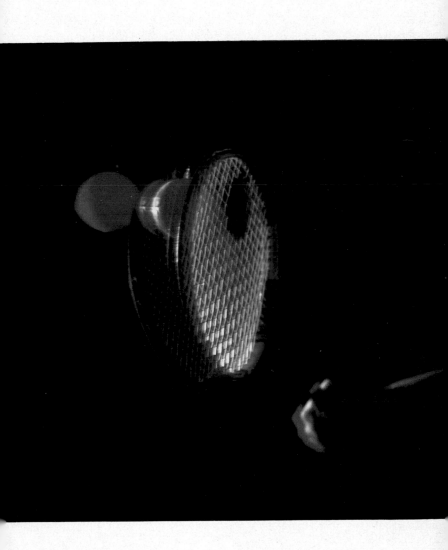

A strobe effect was produced here by firing three flashguns in rapid succession—each flash being separately filtered. Three stages of the rebound are shown on the one frame.

The upper foreground received shadow relief from a clear flashbulb in this shot of a loggia on the Island of Ios. The same scene without the flash fill-in is shown on the left.

A subject in shadow against a brightly-lit background normally produces a silhouette as in the smaller picture. If detail is required a carefully judged flash exposure retains both background brilliance and foreground detail.

A single flash from the left causes the dew drop on the lupin leaf to shine brightly and adds a touch of rim lighting to the leaf.

Shadow relief with reflectors

The use of polished reflectors to provide shadow relief with flash is not to be recommended, inasmuch as it is impossible visually to check the effect.

On the other hand all surfaces which do not specularly reflect light, but diffusely scatter it, are eminently suitable for the relief of shadows in sunlight, tungsten lighting, and especially flash. Such surfaces include white card, projection screens, sheets, tablecloths and bath towels. An almost ideal method of ensuring shadow relief is, where possible, to place the subject close to a whitewashed wall. The intensity of the shadow relief depends on distance between subject and reflector – but not on this alone.

All diffusely reflecting surfaces are capable of brightening quite large subjects. It must not however be overlooked that even the most matt surface tends to reflect the light more in one particular direction. Obliquely incident light is reflected much more directionally than vertically incident light. It must therefore be borne in mind that the lion's share of the reflected light reaches the subject when the lines drawn from the light source and the subject to a point on the reflecting surface at which the light is aimed make equal angles with the plane of the reflecting surface. Light bounces from a point on a flat surface in exactly the same way as a billiard ball rebounds from the cushion – at an angle equal to the angle at which it strikes the surface.

Fortunately this game of billiards with light source and reflector is not to be taken too literally. Despite any preferential reflection the light remains quite well diffused.

If the reflecting surface is not white, but red, blue, yellow or green, the reflected light will of course assume a red, blue, yellow or green tint which it will at once pass on to the shadows of the subject. Coloured shadows often – much too often – inadvertently enter into the picture, and naturally are not specially welcome. On the other hand there are occasions when this very effect can be used as an aid to pictorial composition.

Another quite important factor in the intensity of the fill-lighting is however the distance of the light source from the subject. The nearer the reflecting surface is to the subject and the farther the flash, the greater is the shadow relief

Effects of tele lighting

The intensity with which the shadows in a subject are illuminated by the use of a reflector depend not only on its size, its position in the room, its colour and its distance from the subject, but also on the distance of the flashgun from the subject.

Here we are concerned with one of the three effects of *tele lighting,* or as it is perhaps better termed in this connection *tele flash.* If the flash is set up very close to the subject, there will be very high contrasts in highlight and shadow. If on the other hand by using an extension cable it is taken well back away from the subject the shadows will receive more light. This of course assumes that either we are operating in a room with really light toned walls and a good reflecting ceiling, or, if outdoors, that equivalent reflecting surfaces are available.

It may on the face of it seem surprising that the distance of the light source affects not only the exposure, but also the lighting. The reason for this is that the illumination intensity varies in inverse proportion to the square of the distance, which is the usual, rather confusing way of stating the inverse square law. It might be clearer to say that the illumination varies in inverse proportion to the relationship between the proposed distance and the reference distance. Thus, if we move a lamp from 3 ft to 6 ft from the subject, the distance relationship is 6 : 3 or 2 : 1, the square of which is 4 : 1 which, inversely, is 1 : 4. The illumination is therefore reduced to one quarter. Had we moved the lamp to 8 ft the relationship would be 8 : 3 and the strength would be reduced to 3^2 : 8^2 = about one seventh. Conversely if we moved the lamp to 2ft the light strength would alter in the ratio 3^2 : 2^2, i.e. it would be rather more than doubled.

And now for the practical side: the diagram shows a figure lit from close up by a light source at 3 feet distance. A reflecting surface has been arranged 6 feet to one side. The direct light path of 3 feet thus compares with a flash – white wall – subject reflected light path of 12 feet.

In itself this light path difference of 4 : 1 is quite considerable, but because of the operation of the "inverse square law" the ratio of the resulting illumination intensities becomes 1 : 16. Even ignoring the fact that still furter light is lost at the reflecting surface not

Reflected light. A, Direct plus reflected light with subject close to
wall. B, Card, mirror, metal foil etc used to throw light into face.
C, All-round light from two sources and two reflectors. D, Liberal
fill-in lighting from three reflecting surfaces.

much could be expected from a "fill light" which has only $1/16$ the intensity of the direct flash illumination. And in fact not a trace of it is to be detected in the resulting photograph. But now suppose the light source is taken back to a distance of $22^1/2$ feet from the subject. At once we have a very different state of affairs. The indirect light path via the reflecting wall is now not a great deal longer than the direct path: it is in fact about $28^1/2$ feet. This reduces the ratio of direct and indirect light path to 28.5 : 22.5, or 1.28 : 1, and the ratio of direct to indirect lighting intensity to $1.28^2 : 1^2$ or 1.6 : 1 – a fill lighting which can be seen. Even if there is considerable light loss at the reflecting surface – there is still adequate reserve.

However our example can offer no more than an indication. Fill lighting depends upon so many other things that it is impossible to calculate it with precision, only to estimate it. In practice the effect of tele lighting in illuminating the shadows is often considerably greater than bare theory would lead one to expect.

This is particularly the case where the light source illuminates a very large part of the room, thus causing a bigger area of reflecting surfaces to contribute light to relieving the shadows.

Here flashbulbs are superior to electronic flash, because their much wider light spread illuminates very much more of the walls and ceiling.

The contribution of walls and ceiling to fill lighting can of course, in the case of electronic flash, be augmented by setting the reflector to wide angle coverage or interposing a diffusing disc or a pocket handkerchief to spread the beam.

I have already indicated that with few exceptions "soft" lighting is suitable only for close-ups. Tele flash in a room with light-coloured walls is one of these exceptions. The degree of shadow relief attainable is limited only by the spread of the flash source.

The essential thing about this tele light effect seems to me to lie in the fact that pictures taken with a single flash give the effect of having been taken with several light sources, or at least with one principal source and one or two supplementary lights.

People are much too quick to urge the use of a second and third light source. Instead, every effort should first be made to exhaust all the potentialities of the single source, then, and only then, considering further sources.

124

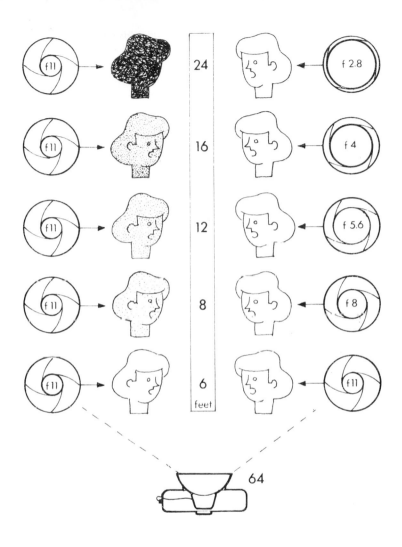

Inverse square law. When the flash distance is doubled, the illumination falls to one quarter. To maintain subject brightness you have to open the lens up two stops. The background 8ft behind a subject 8ft from the camera receives only one quarter of the illumination on the subject.

The attraction of using tele lighting as fill-light should not however prevent us from appreciating that we sometimes actually need strong contrast, bright highlights, black shadows, bringing their enriching quality to the picture whether it be contre jour or rim lighted. For this we need not tele lighting, but its opposite, close-up lighting.

Tele lighting by its nature has quite different properties. To all appearances it is able to set at nought the inverse square law. To be sure, it is commonly taken for granted that a flash photograph can always be recognized as such by the fact that the foreground is brightly lit and the background dark. Nevertheless I have in my collection a large number of flash pictures which do not conform to this pattern. These are either bounce flash or tele flash photographs, and the much greater distance of the light source causes it to penetrate deep into the farthest depths of the subject.

An example will explain the reason for this.

First take the case of a flash gun placed at 3 feet from the subject, with the background 6 feet behind it, and therefore 9 feet from the flash source. The ratio of the two distances flash-subject and flash-background is thus 1 : 3. The lighting contrast is therefore $3^2 : 1^2 = 9 : 1$.

At this low level of illumination the background will come out fairly dark in the picture.

But now suppose the flash gun to be taken farther back, say to 21 feet from the subject; the flash-subject to flash-background ratio now becomes 21 : 27, or barely 1 : 1.3. The lighting contrast thus becomes about 1.65 : 1. The result is that the room appears nicely lighted throughout.

The table opposite shows the change in the ratio of foreground to background lighting intensity as the light source is moved back away from foreground (and background).

If the distance from flash to subject foreground is no greater, or is even less than that from foreground to background, everything behind will be lost in darkness. I once had to take a portrait in a factory workshop with ugly, dirty yellow walls. I deliberately used close-up lighting – i.e. with the flash distance less than the background distance – so that the ugly colour was completely lost in gloom. Naturally I had to put up with a high lighting contrast. On another occasion I used the same technique in the dressing room

EFFECT OF FLASH DISTANCE ON LIGHTING DEPTH

Ratio of flash-foreground distance to subject depth	Ratio of foreground to background lighting intensity
$1/8 \times$	81. $\times$
$1/4 \times$	25. $\times$
$1/2 \times$	9 $\times$
$1 \times$	4 $\times$
$2 \times$	2.25 $\times$
$3 \times$	1.8 $\times$
$4 \times$	1.6 $\times$
$5 \times$	1.4 $\times$
$6 \times$	1.35 $\times$
$7 \times$	1.3 $\times$
$8 \times$	1.27 $\times$
$9 \times$	1.23 $\times$
$10 \times$	1.2 $\times$

of an actress. In this case however as a precaution I used a second light source to relieve shadows on the face.

With increasing distance, the power of the flash to penetrate the depths of the subject rapidly increases; but to this, too, there is a limit. What might be termed an optimum value is reached when the flash source reaches three to four times the distance *in front of* the subject that the background lies *behind* it. Further increase in the flash distance is not accompanied by any sensational gain in lighting penetration.

My own practice is to set up the light source at not more than four times the foreground-background distance in front of the subject. Otherwise I am just wasting light. For the rest I also try so far as possible to use it as top or side lighting; this also has the effect of still further improving the ratio of flash-foreground and flash-background distances.

Moreover when used indoors tele lighting – in conjunction with room reflection – still further reduces light fall off. That is to say, whereas outdoors the calculated values hold quite rigorously, indoors conditions are still a little more favourable for illumination in depth.

Admittedly it is not possible always to fulfil the ideal lighting conditions. I have even set up flash units outside a doorway so that they shone through into the room – all for the sake of tele lighting.

One thing, however, still remains to be dealt with: the third tele light effect.

Close-up and tele lighting can also affect the nature of shadows. As these will be dealt with in the next section, this aspect need not be detailed here.

One other thing: tele lighting can also be employed to achieve uniform lighting when copying pictures, using a single flash source directed from one side.

Effect of light source size

Light sources having extended luminous surfaces produce shadows with undefined edges. Such shadows can be divided into two zones. In the centre is the deep shadow, or *umbra*, untouched by the lighting. The edge of the shadow is termed the *penumbra*, a zone in which light and shadow intermingle. Such a zone exists wherever an appreciable part – but only a part – of the luminous surface of the light source is covered by the object which is throwing the shadow. That part of the light source surface which is not so screened peeps around the edge of the obstructing object and partially illuminates the shadow.

If we imagine the surface of the light source to be made extremely large, the greater part of it will of necessity project beyond the subject, ultimately to the point where the subject can no longer cast any shadow at all. As a result, the shadow disappears – at least, all the central umbra. At the most a soft half shadow will remain.

On the other hand let us assume that we are able to reduce the size of the light source to a mere point, which cannot be covered only partially but, either completely or not at all. The result then is that the shadows formed are sharply outlined, solid "umbra" through and through. All "penumbral" half shadows are completely eliminated.

The statement that a large light source gives soft shadows and a small light source sharp shadows is however not unconditionally true. It is quite true that a very small light source cannot give soft shadows, but on the other hand large light sources can quite well produce sharp shadows. All that is necessary is to remove the light source sufficiently far from the subject. Anything will appear small if it is sufficiently far away. Consequently a large light source if far enough away will act as though it were a minute spot. In general the shadows will be quite pleasantly sharp if its distance from the subject is about 10 to 20 times the diameter of its luminous surface. Ten to 20 times may seem a somewhat wide latitude, but it is in fact very difficult to be precise: for the sharpness of the shadows depends — at least so far as large area light sources are concerned (though not point sources) – not only the light source-subject distance, but also on the distance of the subject from the surface on which the shadow is formed. So far as this latter distance is concerned things are precisely the reverse: the farther away the background, the softer the shadow outlines. This can be effectively demonstrated by placing a ball on the table and lighting it so that it produces a long shadow on the table, somewhat resembling a cigar. Close to the ball the shadow is knife sharp: farther away, it is vaguer.

How far are we interested in absolutely sharp shadows?

I have, for example, projected the shadow of a net on a face, the structure of a waste paper basket on the floor, the coloured shadow of glasses on a tablecloth. But quite apart from special cases of this kind I regard sharply defined shadows, perhaps with some fill lighting, as far more valuable for portraits and group photographs than indefinite shadows.

At one time the only way of keeping flash light sources really small was to remove the reflector or cover it over with black material. This meant a loss of light equivalent to two stops. Nowadays most electronic flash units, and flashbulb flashguns too, are so small in size that they give sharp outline shadows anyway. If a larger illuminating surface should be desired it is always possible to interpose a translucent screen, or recourse may be had to bounce flash (page 84). The illuminated ceiling or wall then becomes a light source in its own right, because it determines the lighting effect and easily disposes of troublesome shadows.

Silhouettes and back lighting

Silhouettes differ from shadows in general inasmuch as an essential feature of silhouettes is a perfectly sharp and undistorted outline. One must however differentiate clearly also between silhouettes and backlit photographs.

When used as back lighting, the flash directly illuminates the whole of the back of the subject – everything that is completely hidden from the camera. For silhouette photography, too, the flash must it is true be likewise hidden behind the camera. The difference however is that for silhouettes it must be turned backwards, away from the subject, so as to light the background only. "Background" here must be understood in a very broad sense, for while it may be just a light coloured wall, it may equally be any brightly lit space. It may be the whole environment of the subject, brightly illuminated, only the subject itself remaining starkly unlighted in the foreground. I have made any number of such silhouette pictures. One quite typical case of a flash silhouette perhaps merits a brief description: It was in Paläa Chora at Aighina. In one of the 27 Byzantine chapels which are a feature of this place I met a student from Athens. She was copying a fresco depicting a saint. His face was typically Byzantine: her profile almost classical in its austerity.

I first of all took a straight flash picture of her, but I was somehow not quite satisfied with it. I was looking for something still more striking and perhaps also still more characteristic of the subject. Accordingly, using an extension cable, I set up my flash on the floor behind her, directly beside her feet. Around it I carefully draped my anorak, which completely screened her from any stray light from the flash, which could have seriously prejudiced the whole effect of the picture. The idea was that the flash should obliquely illuminate only the back wall of the chapel. High contrast document films are useful for silhouette work. It then becomes easy, in subsequent enlarging, to suppress all half-tones, thus reducing the picture to pure black and white.

When taking silhouette photographs at home, for the lighted background I prefer to use not the usual opaque surface but a translucent sheet. I stretch a sheet of translucent paper over, for instance, an open doorway. Behind it, on the end of an extension lead, the flash is set up; in front of it is the subject. The subject is then photographed against the illuminated background. I have frequently used a whole roll of translucent paper in this way, with one end secured to the ceiling with drawing pins, the other hanging free. However, whether incident or transmitted background illumination is used is not all that important. The main thing is to see that there is a *large* illuminated area behind the unlighted subject.

There is every justification for bringing silhouette lighting under the heading of indirect back lighting. Direct back lighting on the other hand – which usually produces a rim of light around the subject – is achieved by the use of a light source of small area, usually not visible in the picture. As a rule in such pictures the background is fairly dark, at least so far as flash back lighting is concerned. In daylight things are rather different because of the bright sky.

The light rim produced by back lighting may be quite narrow, or it may on the other hand be really wide. Three factors enter into this:

1 The position of the light source: If the flash unit is hidden directly behind the subject, it produces a very fine fringe, which however is fairly uniformly distributed all around the subject. If on the other hand the light comes from the side or from above, the fringe is broader, and in this case, depending upon the direction from which it comes, the fringe appears only on one side of the subject.

2 The size of the light source: Small sources give narrow fringes, larger sources broader ones. The effect, however, is not very pronounced, and is really only of theoretical interest. Nevertheless the use of a large area source – flash with a translucent screen – can be quite valuable in so far as it softens wrinkles, or lip creases, which would be heavily emphasized by a small light source.

3 Exposure: The rim, or fringe, of light is not of course uniformly bright throughout its whole breadth. If the exposure is on the short side it is more scanty than with fuller exposure or a larger stop; nevertheless there are some types of fringe which are scarcely affected by varying the exposure.

One general rule holds good for both direct and indirect back lighting: Negative films should be given one stop fuller exposure (but see also page 99).

Reversal film can be given strictly correct exposure, or even slight underexposure, for silhouette pictures. For back lighting, the lens should be closed down a further stop. It is important to remember that in silhouette pictures the exposure must be determined by the distance from light source to background.

Sometimes a silhouette which has received some 2 to 3 stops overexposure gives a quite extravagant effect. The subject no longer appears completely black, and takes on a kind of tracing character. In the case of colour film this is usually accompanied by a colour cast derived from the nearby room decoration. Incidentally silhouette photographs need not necessarily be devoid of colour interest. This may be introduced into the background by way of a rug, or a large colour design. And again there are all the many attractive transparent or translucent objects, from a glass of red wine to a yellow flower or a green scarf. All such colour comes out in a silhouette photograph. It is just in this matter of transparency and translucency that direct and indirect back lighting differ in their essential character. Typical examples might be a goblet of pure transparent bright red wine and a glass of cloudy natural orange juice. The translucent orange juice lights up brightly in back lighting, but loses its lustre in silhouette lighting. Before an illuminated background a goblet of wine glows uniformly red, the rim of the glass appearing as a soft black line. In direct back lighting this appears as a bright line of light against a black background, and the wine itself exhibits only one or two red spots of light. Only when the lighting conditions are particularly favourable is a shimmer to be seen over the whole goblet.

The behaviour of tobacco smoke is interesting. Against a bright background it forms black clouds which come out clearly only with very short exposure. Back lighting produces bright, shining clouds against a black background. But in one's enthusiasm for these striking light effects do not forget to use a lens hood.

Indirect lighting techniques

We have already discussed bounced flash with the flash unit on the camera. A flash unit independent of the camera can in some cases, however, give better lighting quality.

Take the case in which, for some reason, the camera must be kept close to the subject. Fixed firmly in the accessory shoe, the upward tilted flash unit would result in too much top lighting. It is better in such a case to remove the flash from the camera and fix it up somewhere well behind the camera, maybe (with the aid of one of those very convenient camera clamps, or "clampods") to the back of a chair, the edge of a table, or a door handle. Once a suitable position has been found from which the flash can be directed obliquely upward, with the camera in the hand and an extension cable pictures can be taken of any point in the room. The brightness will be sufficiently uniform throughout. The question of exposure has already been dealt with on page 87. So far, bounce flash has been described as depending on reflection from the ceiling, but this by no means has to be the case. There are times when such ceiling reflection is impracticable – in particular when the ceiling is not light enough in tone, when it is strongly coloured, or when it is too high. There was the occasion when Japanese dolls were on view in the Hamburg "Planten un Bloomen" exhibition grounds. I was so impressed by these delicate creations from Nippon that I flashed away wildly in all directions. One of these mini-ladies I particularly wanted to photograph by the most delicate lighting – and this meant indirect flash. Unfortunately the ceiling of the hall was of dark wood. The walls, it is true, were light in tone, but much too far away to enable me to use them for bounce flash. By good fortune I was wearing a sufficiently white shirt. Off came my jacket and I secured my indirect lighting by directing the flash against my body from about a foot away. This "shirt-bounce" light retains its "softening" character up to a distance of 3 to 5 feet. It is only practicable therefore for close-ups and large scale portraits. As a basis for exposure, use the combined distance flash-shirt-subject as basis for determining the stop and open up the aperture by about a further $1\frac{1}{2}$ to 2 stops.

In the case of the Japanese doll I had to sacrifice yet a further stop, since there was no reflection from walls and ceiling. The lighting which resulted from this set-up was a "soft frontal lighting". In connection with this type of lighting it must be pointed out that for distances greater than 5 feet the reflectors, to be effective, must comprise large surfaces – such as white walls, not small cards – and these must be directly behind the camera. From the point of view of lighting quality, this soft frontal lighting constitutes an enhancement of direct frontal lighting – and a very considerable enhancement. It is, in fact, the most flattering lighting that it is possible to obtain. Wrinkles and creases, and other blemishes which can occur in a portrait, are smoothed out in quite a unique manner, while at the same time retaining, considerably better than is possible with direct frontal lighting, the modelling of the subject. There is, of course, no outlining cast shadow with this lighting.

It is true that light reflected from the ceiling softly floods the subject in the same way, but in this case there still remain shadows in the deepest clefts, especially when bounce lighting comes too steeply from above, when it can make creases and wrinkles painfully obvious.

Even worse is a direct top lighting, which has an ageing effect on the model. The flattering indirect frontal lighting on the other hand takes at least a decade off the apparent age of a well preserved woman in her forties.

Needless to say, a large sheet of translucent paper in front of, but not too close to the light source serves the same purpose as the roundabout lighting provided by a diffuse reflecting surface – but bounce frontal lighting is in practice much easier to set up.

Incidentally I have shut off whole corners of exhibition rooms with a strip of translucent paper. Metallic works of art, which by direct flash lighting were ever prone to become unmanageable with reflections, were then set up in the corner for photographing. Illumination was provided by flash from outside through the translucent sheet, the camera viewing through a hole in it.

On another occasion a showcase of gold jewellery was surrounded completely with translucent paper and illuminated with two flash units. The exhibits thus lay under, so to speak, a light tent. Personally, for light tent photography I prefer to use tungsten lamps, but it is not always possible to do so on account of their dependence upon mains connection.

Finally there is the possibility of semi-indirect flash. This can be especially useful in cases where the light source is rather inadequate for fully indirect lighting. For this, the flash is, as usual, directed obliquely upward towards the ceiling, but not so far as to prevent a certain amount of light from the lower edge of the reflector from shining direct on to the subject. The main part of the light thus travels the usual indirect way via the ceiling. This results in an intermediate type of lighting between direct and indirect, which can yet be relied upon to give good illumination of the shadows.

The exposure is calculated as usual from the guide number or looked up in a table, but the lens is then opened up by 1 to 1^1/$_2$ stops beyond the indicated value. Admittedly some experience is necessary in judging the best angle at which to tilt the flash, but semi-indirect lighting should not be cold shouldered on this account, because it really is most effective in softening facial defects – even more so than the original straight bounce lighting.

Flash in the Chinese lantern

Flash units today are fortunately so small and compact that they can readily be concealed in an ordinary table lamp, a lantern, or any other light fixture.

Only in exceptional cases do I remove the reflector from a flash gun. Almost always, however, I wrap it loosely in two layers of tissue paper. This improves the distribution of the light, and also eliminates any danger that the flash bulb itself will be imaged as an all too brilliant spot of light.

Here it is not possible to determine exposure from the guide number. Using the AG 3 B or the AG 1 with a 50 ASA (18 DIN) colour film, I stop down to f22 and as a precaution take another shot at f32.

The lantern itself always comes out extraordinarily bright, but the surroundings are but dimly illuminated. This must be borne in mind, if the results are not to prove disappointing.

If the face of a child holding such a Chinese lantern is to be really well lighted, its nose will have to be almost touching the lantern. This can however be overcome by placing a flash unit on the base of the lantern so that the reflector throws the light upwards through the hole, lighting the face of the child bending over it. A useful expedient in this situation is the use of a second flash unit as a silhouette or back light.

Using mirrors with independent flash

For taking pictures through the mirror, frontal flash (page 76) is in itself completely adequate. Bounce flash is also perfectly suitable.

There is however a third method, using a flash gun triggered from the camera, which is not entirely without interest, and this because, among other reasons, it is possible with it to illuminate effectively small, and even minute mirrors. I have already mentioned that in these cases certain difficulties arise with frontal lighting mirror pictures.

The flash source has simply to be placed beside, above, or below the mirror. It then illuminates your own face — assuming your intention is to produce a mirror image of yourself — or that of some other person. In either case the face in question appears brightly illuminated in the mirror. Exposure is determined purely by the flash-subject distance, measured as before via the mirror. Under normal conditions the frontal lighting method would appear to be by far the better, the mirror image appearing as though the subject were lighted by two independent light sources. Although the independent mirror technique cannot be compared with it, I would not wholly decry it. Only by this method is it possible to emulate all the effects possible to a distorting mirror. To mention just a few from the wealth of natural mirrors around us. Christmas tree ornaments, polished metal vases, bent polished metal foils, spoons, soup ladles, and so forth.

The flash to subject distance is more conveniently measured with the reflex viewfinder or rangefinder of the camera.

One point should be mentioned here, and that is that it is not enough to consider only the mirror image when taking through-the-mirror photographs. Thus for instance a model may be holding a hand mirror the back of which is presented to the camera. The single flash which is used to light the scene, also shines direct on to the model giving an additional lateral back lighting. This light is reflected by the mirror, maybe right into her face, where it appears as a bright spot.

It is interesting to consider how it is possible to produce such a spot effect with controlled precision. There are two possible ways: The model adjusts the angle of the mirror until she can see in it the flashgun in the background with both eyes; alternatively the operator on his part can adjust the position of the flashgun so that from its position he can see in the mirror precisely the spot on the model's face at which he wishes the light spot to appear.

The mobile flash

The next part of this book is devoted to the use of a number of flash sources. However it is possible with a single mobile flash-gun to achieve a lighting effect equivalent to that produced by a whole arsenal of separate light sources. The method is simply to fire a number of successive flashes at the same subject – which needless to say must not, in the meantime, move or alter in any way. Where, in practice, can this mobile flash technique be used to advantage? Take the case of photographing a marble statue. This could be done at midnight at new moon, with the light out and the curtains drawn, making a number of exposures with the single flash from different directions with the camera shutter left open on the T setting. If a large-format technical camera were used, which of course has no double exposure prevention device, the open flash method could be dispensed with. All that would be necessary would be to make a number of flash exposures on the same film at any suitable shutter speed. Naturally, the camera must be securely mounted on a tripod, and a stable one at that. When this latter method is used, the possibility of stray light caus-ing trouble is not so important as when using the open flash technique. Be that as it may, this residual stray light, be it daylight or artificial light, must be reduced to the utmost minimum. A friend of mine fell right into such a case head first with drums beating and trumpets sounding!

He had been commissioned to photograph a conference room. The room was full of sunshine. He accordingly set his camera to f8 and 1/250 sec., which was the fastest shutter speed available on his technical camera. Unfortunately his electronic flash unit needed a stop of f4 to light the whole room adequately. So – he reasoned – I'll give it four successive flashes at f8: that will amount to the same thing! The reader will probably already have jumped to the fallacy in this argument. The obtrusive daylight also will have been given four times the exposure. Believe me, I had never before seen such overexposure in a window frame!

In rooms in which there are windows, mobile flash can only be used at night. With this proviso, however, it is one of the most valuable of techniques for providing adequate lighting for church naves and the like. Its main application is in fact to interior architectural photography, using the procedure: Put out all lights, open the shutter, give *one* flash to every part of the room, and *more than one* only to such areas as are too far away. Exposure is of course determined in exactly the same way as if an equivalent number of individual light sources had been used. In the case of areas which are too far away, the distance from flash to area must be divided by the distance for which the stop has been calculated. The result, multiplied by itself, gives the number of flashes required for this particular area.

But it has to be remembered that one flash at f2 gives more effective exposure than 16 flashes at f8. This is due to the intermittency effect which occurs with non-continuous exposures. The same quantity of light, when administered in one "dose", has more effect upon sensitive material than when given "in instalments".

In my own practice, if the number of flashes required does not exceed 12 I give one extra flash for each 4 flashes. If more than 12 flashes are needed, then I give an extra flash for every 2. I should however point out that I have experimented with only one type of colour reversal film. Other materials may possibly not behave in this fashion. Incidentally, between each two flash exposures, each of which is carefully aimed at the centre of some particular area, the position of the flash unit should always be slightly altered, thus tending to avoid cast shadows which should not be permitted to haunt mobile flash pictures.

And one thing more: I am fully aware that a flash lighted room with black window panes is not always specially attractive. We have already seen how daylight entering through the windows can introduce difficulties which are almost insuperable. However there is a way out: Overnight, carry out the whole mobile flash operation, but do *not* finally close the shutter (unless of course there is no double exposure prevention device on the camera). For preference, close the lens with a lens cap. In the dim light of daybreak, remove the lens cap briefly.

138

Flash with
Two or
More Sources

The following little experiment is worth making: Insert a small flashbulb in your flashgun. Now with adhesive cellulose tape stick a second bulb in contact with it. When the first bulb is fired, you will find that the second bulb also fires.

If you are a user of flash cubes, the experiment can be made still more striking: remove the transparent casing from a flash cube, and then remove also the metal foil stamped with the reflectors from the tiny bulbs. If one of the bulbs is fired all the remaining three will likewise ignite.

There is, of course, nothing really to be gained in light output by this "sympathetic triggering" technique, because the little reflectors are no longer performing their proper function. There are in fact a whole range of other possible expedients which will better achieve this purpose. You can for instance use

1 A faster film
2 A double flash head
3 A more powerful flash bulb
4 A number of successive flashes by the mobile flash technique (page 137).
5 Two or more flash heads.

This last method is in my opinion only very rarely employed merely in order to increase the light output. It is usually rather a matter of improving the quality of the lighting. The simplest way is to use two flash heads on the camera, each of which is fired from one of the two flash contacts. On the Leica, I connect the main lamp to the contact marked with the lightning symbol: the second lamp is then connected to the contact marked with a lamp symbol. (As in this latter case the whole output of the flashbulb is not utilized, this flashgun should be relegated to the role of a subsidiary light source.)

Generally, but not always, cameras with between-lens shutters have only one flash connection. Nevertheless this can be used to trigger a number of flashguns with the help of a multi-way connector.

Assuming, now, that the usual flashguns are employed, using 22.5, 15, or 6 volt batteries, it is essential, in coupling two or more flashguns, to observe the following three rules:

1 Use only flash guns having the same voltage battery. (It is best, if possible, to couple together only flashguns of the same type.) If a 22.5 V and a 15 V flashgun, or a 15 V and a 6 V, or even a 6 V and a 22.5 V, were coupled together, the flashbulb would fire on insertion. The "state of charge" of the batteries in the two flashguns to be coupled should not be too different. Also the polarity must be the same when connected. That is to say, the batteries must be lying in the same direction in their receptacles.

2 First of all insert the bulbs, and only then connect the two flashguns together. If the procedure is reversed and the flashguns connected first, the bulbs will fire on insertion. Even if after the first exposure fresh bulbs have to be inserted, each flashgun must first be again disconnected before inserting the flashbulb.

3 Up to three flashguns can be coupled together in this way without overloading the camera contact.

Some 15 volt flashguns have 100 μF, some 200 μF capacitors. In the first case as many as six flashguns may be connected to the camera contact without risk of overloading. In the latter only three. Six-volt flashguns are normally fitted with 250 μF capacitors. As a result these have not sufficient power to provide reliable triggering over the more extensive circuits required by multiflash operation. For these, therefore, it is advisable to use 15 or 22.5 volt flashguns or alternatively make use of a slave unit.

In order to avoid unnecessary wastage of flashbulbs, it is much the best plan to make use of test bulbs when first carrying out coupling tests.

It does not matter in the least what types of flashbulbs are simultaneously triggered in a multi-flash circuit.

In cameras which are provided with two separate flash connections, the two circuits are completely independent of one another, so that three flashguns can be operated from each contact. For this reason, such cameras permit the simultaneous use of two different systems – one contact being devoted to, say, 22.5 volt flashguns, the other to 15 volts.

A simple, practical and convenient method of operating a multi-flash system is the photocell "slave unit". Most types respond to the light impulse of a flashbulb, even if perhaps not quite so promptly as to electronic flash, and they are also equipped to

EQUIPMENT FOR FLASH WITH SEVERAL SOURCES

Lighting set-up and connections	Auxiliary equipment required
Two flash heads on camera with one flash contact	Two-way or multi-way connector (or cable with multi-way outlet) and at least one extension cable or photocell
Three flash heads on camera with one flash contact	Three-way connector (or cable with multi-way outlet) and at least two extension cables or a photocell with at least two output connections
Two flash heads on camera with two flash connections	One or two extension cables
Three flash heads on camera with two flash connections	One two-way connector (or cable with multi-way outlet) and 2 or 3 extension cables (or photocell and 1 or 2 cables)
Six flash heads on camera with two flash connections	Two three-way connectors (or two cables with multi-way outlet) and 5 to 6 extension cables (or alternatively a photocell slave equipment)
Simplest type of camera with built-in flash	A camera release flash triggering adapter or photocell slave equipment, with any necessary cables

trigger flashbulbs. This useful device enables one or more additional flash sources to be brought into operation even in the case of cameras with built-in flash.

Simultaneous firing of electronic flash units

First we must distinguish between two different types of unit. The one type is specially equipped to enable an extra flash head to be directly connected, and in some cases up to six or seven such flash heads. The other type is designed specifically for sole use. The additional flash heads in their turn also fall into two cate-

142

SIMULTANEOUS TRIGGERING OF SEVERAL ELECTRONIC FLASH UNITS

Electronic flash equipment connected to the X contact of the camera	Auxiliary equiment required
Electronic flash unit with facility for connecting additional flash heads	Additional flash heads or slave equipment with self-contained flash head
Two matched electronic flash units	A two-way or multi-way connector (or cable with multi-way outlet) with appropriate cable or photocell
Different types of electronic flash unit which cannot be coupled together	A camera release flash triggering adapter and appropriate cable connections

SIMULTANEOUS TRIGGERING OF FLASH BULBS AND ELECTRONIC FLASH

Type of camera	Auxiliary equipment
Cameras with at least two flash connections (e. g. Leica, Leica-flex, single-lens Rollei, Exakta Varex). The electronic flash unit is connected to the X contact, and the flash bulb – or flashbulbs – to the F contact	Two connecting cables (if several flash units have to be connected to one contact suitable multi-way connectors or a cable with a multi-way outlet) or a photocell slave equipment which responds to a flash bulb or can be used to trigger it
Cameras with only one contact	Flash bulbs are triggered by a camera release flash triggering adapter, or better by a slave unit
Cameras with built-in flash	Slave unit to trigger electronic flash

gories – the simple flash head as such, and those with their own capacitor. As the capacity of the capacitor is the primary factor determining the light output of an electronic flash unit, one thing will be quite obvious: if the simple type of flash head, without separate capacitor, is used, the output of the main unit has to be split up among all the auxiliary flash heads. Thus three such flash

143

heads will only give out about the same quantity of light as a single one would have done. The other type of flash heads, with built-in capacitors can – although they need not necessarily – be as powerful as the central unit. This again depends on the capacity of their individual capacitors. They have however the indisputable advantage that their output is completely independent of the main unit, whose own output remains unaffected.

Some flash units on the market have provision for only one additional flash head, others for several. Yet other units are equipped for the attachment of both simple flash heads and flash heads complete with their own capacitors.

But how about the electronic flash units which have no provision at all for supplementary flash heads? There is no question of making use of a second flash contact on the camera, because electronic flash must of necessity be connected to the X contact, and this is rarely found in duplicate. Can two flashes be simply connected up to the single contact via a two-way connector?

I put this point to a number of manufactures of electronic flash equipment, and the following is an extract from the replies which I received:

Robert Bosch Elektronik und Photokino GmbH:

... on principle we do not advise the use of multi-way connectors ... it has to be borne in mind that the circuitry of electronic flash triggering differs widely from model to model, and this can even result in failure to operate, as for example when in one unit the negative pole of the capacitor is connected to earth and in the other unit the positive pole. We have in fact established that even flash units of the same type, that is to say with the same triggering circuitry, do not necessarily operate perfectly in parallel. Also there is the matter of the greater load on the synchronizing contact of the camera.

Metz Apparatewerke:

The multi-way coupling connectors for synchronizing cables which are commercially available do as a rule permit the synchronizing cables of two or three electronic flash units to be connected together, so that all of them can be simultaneously triggered by the synchronizing contact of the camera. However an essential condition for reliable triggering of the units thus coupled is that the triggering voltage should be the same on all the synchronizing cables. All Mecablitz flash units have the same trig-

144

gering voltage, namely 250 V, and may therefore be connected together without hesitation. On the other hand this parallelling of the triggering circuits of the flash units puts a considerably greater load on the synchronizing contact of the camera shutter than is the case with the triggering of a single flash unit, thus tending to wear it out more quickly. For this reason this combined triggering expedient should be confined to only occasional use.

Braun, Frankfurt:
In our experience the connecting together of flash equipment of the same type or make is on principle not to be recommended. We have established that even with a flash unit of unaltered type the triggering voltage is occasionally quite manifestly altered during the currency of a series ... So far as our own products are concerned we can only say that all models may be interconnected, irrespective of type and year of manufacture.

Agfa:
In the case of electronic flash equipment, DIN 19014 lays down a limiting value which normally may not be exceeded. The connecting together of a number of electronic flash units by way of a multi-way connector would cause this limit to be exceeded by, for example a factor of two in the case of two units, while with three units it is even three times exceeded, which may lead to damage or destruction of the flash contact in the camera. This danger of damage to the flash synchronizing contact is further accentuated when there is a tendency on the part of the contacts to rebound.

From these opinions we must conclude that electronic flash units of the same type may, *as a makeshift expedient,* be coupled together. How long the camera synchronizing contact will stand up to the increased load is subject to neither rule nor guarantee. An alternative method which has again and again been recommended is that of "wireless" remote control via a photocell. The experience which I had previously gathered with three different older types of equipment were so catastrophic that at that time I deprecated its use: I considered it to be practicable only when the equipment could be firmly mounted on a stand and used in the studio – or at least an improvised studio. However a few experiments with more recent equipment completely converted me. This new equipment reacts to reflected light from the subject, and indeed even to bounce flash, so that it is no longer necessary to aim the receiver photocell accurately in the direction of the primary triggering source. Thus it becomes easily possible to use a photocell-triggered multi-flash set-up in really tough reportage situations, in circumstances wherein the "wireless" connection between main and "slave" flash units represents a real advantage. However on occasions when photocell triggering has to be used without previous test (page 196) with a between-lens shutter, the shutter speed used should not be faster than 1/125 sec. In the case of focal plane shutters it is better to use one stop longer exposure times.

For the rest: photocell slave equipment – some types at least – permits synchronous triggering of mixed flashbulbs and electronic flash. This is otherwise possible only with cameras which have two separate flash connections. As an improvised expedient this can also be effected with a camera release flash triggering adapter. (Some interesting tricks with photocells will be found on page 196).

Exposure for uni-directional flash

It would be natural to assume that the addition of a second flash head, a third, fourth, fifth and so on, would in every case so improve the original lighting that the lens could be further stopped down or the light sources removed to a greater distance from the subject. Whether, or to what extent, this is actually the case in practice depends on the way in which the additional lights are placed. The maximum increase in intensity of the lighting results from shining all the lights on to the subject from the same direction. This can be seen in more precise detail from the table on page 147. This is based on the assumption that no illuminating axis differs from any other by an angle greater than 30°. The light sources are all placed close together and serve no other purpose but to increase the intensity of the illumination so far as possible. Already we have willy nilly been confronted with the fact, on numerous occasions, that the illumination intensity falls off as the square of the distance from the light source; nevertheless the consequences of this in practice – at least in my experience – are frequently surprising. Thus if we double the light intensity on our

EXPOSURE ADJUSTMENT FOR ADDITIONAL FLASH HEADS

Number of lamps	Exposure decrease (stops)	or	Increase lamp distance	or	Multiply guide number by
1	–		–		–
2	1		1.4 ×		1.4
3	1½		1.7 ×		1.7
4	2		2 ×		2
6	2½		2.5 ×		2.5
8	3		2.8 ×		2.8
9	3		3 ×		3
12	3½		3.5 ×		3.5

subject by adding another light and go to compensate it by taking the lights further back, it is not twice the distance that will be required, but only 1.4 times. Again if our subject at 5 ft distance is correctly exposed with a stop of f11, and we then move back to 15 ft, or three times the distance, it is not just three times the light that will be needed to compensate. To stop down to between f8 and f5.6 would mean heavy underexposure – in fact f4 would be required, because it is the square of three, that is nine times, the light that will be needed to light the subject to the same intensity at the increased distance of 15 ft. Looked at another way, if we want to keep our stop of f11, we shall need nine light sources instead of the original one.

Thus the inverse square law somewhat drastically limits our field of action. From the other point of view, however, it helps us when it comes to bringing the lights nearer to the subject. For example, when using four AG 3 B flashbulbs and an 800 ASA film a subject calls for f2 at a distance of 260 ft (this takes into account that there is no room reflection out of doors at night). Should we have only two flashbulbs available, the distance must be reduced, not to 130 ft, but only to 185 ft.

The guide number can of course be increased not by adding to the number of lamps but by using a higher speed film. Doubling the ASA speed of the film increases the guide number by a factor of 1.4; four times the speed doubles the guide number; eight times the film speed means 2.8 times the guide number, 16 times film speed 4 times guide number and so on.

The whole picture will perhaps be clarified by the table below, in which both Continental (DIN) and ASA values are set out. The table starts out from the basis of one AG 3 B flashbulb giving a guide number of 92 with a 50 ASA film. At f2.8 the subject distance is then 33 feet. The effect of adding more AG 3 B flashbulbs or faster film will then be seen from the table.

GUIDE NUMBER AND FILM SPEED RELATIONSHIPS

Number of flash bulbs	Film speed ASA	DIN	Stop	Subject distance feet	metres	Guide number feet	metres
1	50	18	f 2.8	33	10	92	28
2 or 1	50 100	18 21	f 2.8	46	14	132	40
			f 4	33	10	132	40
4 or 1 or 2	50 200 100	18 24 21	f 5.6	33	10	185	56
			f 2.8	66	20	185	56
			f 4	46	14	185	56

If an electronic flash unit is used with an additional flash head which has no power pack of its own, then as we have seen the output of the main unit will be halved. The light which was originally radiated by the one lamp is now distributed between two. So far as exposure is concerned, it is immaterial whether the main flash unit is used at full output or the auxiliary flash head is brought in and both aimed at the same part of the subject from the same direction.

Let us suppose that it is required to operate the flash at a considerable distance from the subject and that this means calling in all the flash units available. These will undoubtedly differ widely in their guide numbers. The ultimate effective guide number for the whole lighting assembly can however be calculated from the formula

$$L = \sqrt{L_1{}^2 + L_2{}^2 + L_3{}^2 + \ldots}$$

where L is the required guide number, and L_1, L_2, L_3... are the individual guide numbers of the additional flash heads.

In the case where a number of flash units, of equal or differing power are used to light the subject from the same direction but from different distances, the procedure is first to calculate what would be the correct stop for each unit if used on its own. These are then squared and added together and the square root of the sum gives the required combined guide number:

$$f_n = \sqrt{f_1{}^2 + f_2{}^2 + f_3{}^2 + \ldots}$$

where f_n = the f-number to which the stop must finally be set, and f_1, f_2, f_3 and so on are the individual f-numbers for each unit used on its own.

If the existing daylight or artificial light is sufficiently bright to take into account, the appropriate f-number can be included as one of the terms in the summation.

Finally, for completeness, it may be pointed out that the formula already quoted can be simplified in the case of a number of similar flash units all directed on to the same subject from the same distance. It then becomes:

$$L_n = L_1 \cdot \sqrt{n}$$

where L_1 = guide number for each of the individual lights, and
    n = the number of lights.

There are two sides to everything – at least two, one might well say! Thus we may look at the exposure problem from another angle. Instead of having to determine the stop required for a specified number of flash units, we may for instance want to know how many flash units are required.

This is even easier to calculate: Multiply the distance in feet by the stop, and divide the product by the guide number for a single flash unit; finally multiply this last result by itself. Expressed as a formula:

$$\left(\frac{a \times f}{L}\right)^2 = n$$

where a = distance in feet, f = stop, L = guide number for a single flash source, and n = number of flash heads required

One further tip: It is best from the outset to allow for the absence of room reflections by increasing the value of f in the equation by the equivalent of closing down the aperture by one stop further (in the case of electronic flash $\frac{1}{2}$ stop). This last formula, which I regard as the most important, can also be made use of for determining the number of flashes needed in a "mobile" flash set-up (page 137).

Exposure for omni-directional flash

The purpose of using a number of flash heads is, in the great majority of cases, to improve the quality of the lighting effect. To achieve this, however, the various flash heads must be aimed at the subject from different directions.
Such flash set-ups have two basic aims:

1 To illuminate the whole room (or to light subjects of very large area).
2 To light smaller objects (mostly three-dimensional).

The techniques which we employ for lighting a large space are closely related to the "mobile" flash method (page 137). Every section of the space is individually lighted. First of all, the stop must be decided upon. Assuming that a variety of flash units, with differing guide numbers, have to be used, each guide number must be divided by this stop. The figure obtained in each case determines the distance at which that particular flash unit must be set up from that part of the subject which it is to illuminate. If in any case the distance is such that it cannot be coped with by a single flash head, additional units are brought in.
If, however, the subject is illuminated by flash coming from all directions, in most cases only the main lighting need be taken into account. Only in two cases does the subsidiary lighting play even a subsidiary role in the exposure:

1 Where two equally powerful light sources illuminate a subject from an equal distance and the angle between their directions does not exceed 30°, the illumination intensity is increased by the equivalent of one stop.

2 If the angle between the two sources lies between about 40°
and 80°, the increase in illumination intensity is the equivalent of
half a stop.

These two rules are really all that is necessary. The list of auxiliary
lighting set-ups which have little or no effect on the exposure as
determined by the main source is considerably longer. No additional stopping down is required when:

1 The angle between the main lighting and the auxiliary lights is
greater than 80°.
2 The auxiliary lighting takes the form of back lighting.
3 The second light source used is only half as powerful as the
main light or less.
4 The second light source, although of equal power, is more than
1 1/2 times as far from the subject as the main light.
5 The second light source is dimmed (by interposing a handkerchief or filter or by removing the reflector).
6 The second light source is directed against the ceiling to give
bounce lighting or against a fill-light reflector.

Where a considerable number of flash sources are used, care
should be taken that two or three of them do not add up to compete with the main source. On principle, I recommend that the
main source should unmistakably play the leading role in the
lighting set-up. This obviates any problem with *exposure*. So far
as *lighting quality* is concerned, this course can only be to its advantage. (For the use of computer flash equipment see page 46).

Snapshots with two or three sources

It may sound unbelievable, but it is nevertheless true that it is
possible to take actual flash snapshots with two, or even three separate flash sources provided the situation is not altogether too
tumultuous. I have made the most thoroughgoing tests of suitable techniques on stage, and dance floor, for sport and close-up.
As a rule I hold the most powerful light free in my hand, but admittedly it is more convenient when I can find someone who is kind

enough to act as lighting assistant. The second flash head is slipped into the accessory shoe of my camera, and has no other function but to relieve the shadows cast by the main light. I say "relieve" advisedly, for it must not on any account be permitted to do more than this: it must not be strong enough to modify either the lighting effect or the exposure. To ensure this, I cover the whole reflector of this flash head with a handkerchief. The same effect can be achieved – where this is possible – by removing or folding up the reflector.

If conditions are such as to permit bounce lighting, I tilt this camera-mounted auxiliary flash upwards, keeping the main flash exactly as it was. Since quite a lot of light is always lost in bounce flash, it is permissible in this exceptional case to use the more powerful light source as auxiliary. On occasion I even mount two flash heads on my camera trained on the ceiling.

These two-lamp techniques are – strictly speaking – not a bit more complicated than the use of a single off-the-camera flash. The twin light technique is particularly useful where it is necessary to provide really good relief to the shadows to ensure very low lighting contrast; but above all frontal auxiliary lighting is of value where there is absolutely no room reflection, so that otherwise the shadows are lost in inky blackness. This danger is particularly acute outdoors at night, in large halls and in close-ups. In such circumstances only fill lighting can enable us to make free use of our main flash source as top or under lighting, as side, rim, or even backlighting. Even when I have a close-up light to subdue an obtrusive background, the auxiliary flash does not produce too harsh shadows. Provided the subject distance is not too great I sometimes find it convenient to bring in a third source for flash snapshots. This is used as back lighting, and has of course to be held by an assistant.

Setting up the lights

It is surprising how frequently one reads misleading recommendations for the use of a number of light sources. Thus it is often suggested that the main flash should come from one side of the subject and an auxiliary source light it from the other.

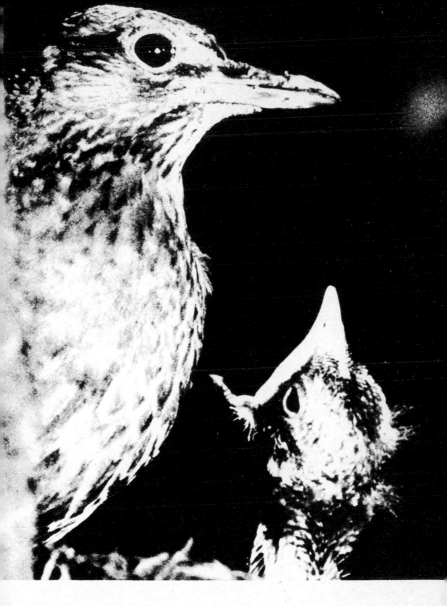

Thrushes shot from a distance with a long-focus lens. The flash necessarily being also distant, a fast film was used to compensate for the weakness of the light reaching the subject.

The soft texture of animal fur is best brought out by plenty of frontal light to soften the shadows from the modelling light, which must come from well to one side—*L Schuster*.

This villainous-looking result came from almost direct frontal lighting very close in. The texture of fur and tongue are brought out by the excess of light penetrating every crevice —*R F Miles*.

For this shot of a performer from the Yugoslav National Ballet, a flash was placed among the footlights, allowing an exposure short enough to virtually kill the overhead lighting on the stage.

This characteristic impression of Marcel Marceau, the mime artist, was obtained with a single flash placed to the left and a little above the level of the head.

A little forethought can improve the picture. If the subject only partially opens the door and puts her head round, the flash illuminates the wall and throws her shadow on to it. Let her open the door wider and stand in the opening so that the flash travels farther past her and darkens the background.

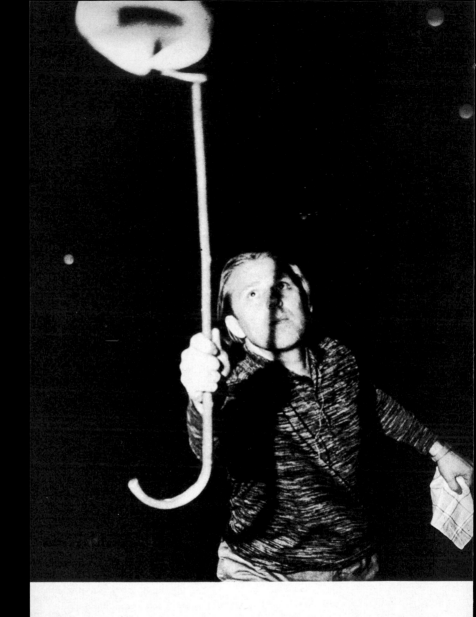

Again the useful flash position off to one side and slightly above head level—this time to catch Russian master clown Oleg Popow in mid-act.

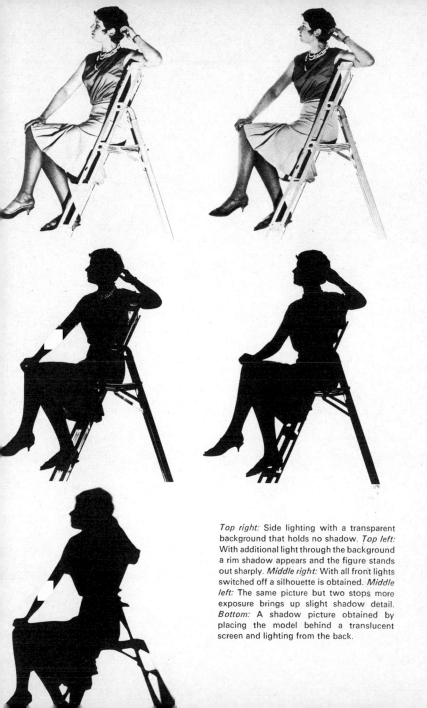

Top right: Side lighting with a transparent background that holds no shadow. *Top left:* With additional light through the background a rim shadow appears and the figure stands out sharply. *Middle right:* With all front lights switched off a silhouette is obtained. *Middle left:* The same picture but two stops more exposure brings up slight shadow detail. *Bottom:* A shadow picture obtained by placing the model behind a translucent screen and lighting from the back.

A single flash at top left is bounced off the background to backlight the cigarette smoke and make it stand out from the unlit part of the background.

This can all too easily result in the formation of objectionable double shadows.

Now it may well be asked whether it really is all that important to avoid double shadows, and if so, why? The reason is that one's natural instinct is to judge the quality of lighting against the background of natural sunlight. And sunlight produces only one shadow. (If one thinks of it, it is curious that we do react in this way, because in the rooms in which we live and work there are usually quite a number of lamps, which cast a corresponding multiplicity of shadows.)

Perfect lighting quality is best achieved – whether it be flash or tungsten lighting – by the combined use of four types of lighting:

1 *The main light:* Here it must first be decided how the main light is to be used: whether as a lateral top lighting, as deep rim lighting or as out-and-out back lighting. The arrangement of the main lighting is the determining factor in the whole effect.

2 *The fill-lighting:* The next decision to be taken is whether fill lighting is wanted at all or whether high contrast lighting is to be preferred. Even if fill lighting is needed it may well be that if the main light is far enough back from the subject it will itself introduce sufficient room reflection. The possible sources of fill lighting are:

(a) Direct flash-on-camera frontal lighting. This will usually have to be dimmed, if it is not to prove too powerful.

(b) Indirect flash-on-camera frontal lighting. (A white surface illuminated behind the camera or a flash gun with a large translucent screen in front of it).

(c) Bounce flash via the ceiling. It may on occasion be expedient to use a number of such sources for a specially intense fill lighting.

None of these methods can result in the formation of double shadows.

3 *Background lighting:* Here it has to be decided whether the subject is to be separated from the background by appropriate lighting techniques or whether it is to be allowed to blend into it. If the background itself is brightly lit, the subject will appear clearly outlined against it, giving a silhouette effect. A dark toned subject against a dark toned background can be isolated from its

surroundings by the use of one or two flash sources used as back lighting.

4 *Effect lighting:* Finally it must be decided whether the picture can be still further improved by the use of any special type of lighting. This might take the form of a flash source concealed within an ordinary lighting fitting. Another possibility lies in specially lit tobacco smoke or red shimmer of wine in a glass.

Colour
Effects
with Flash

Electronic flash when used with daylight reversal film gives a colour rendering similar to high altitude sunshine. Older flashguns in particular sometimes gave a rather cool tone. Blue flashbulbs on the other hand give slightly warm toned colour transparencies. Small flashbulbs give a colour rendering more comparable with late afternoon sunshine. Red and yellow are brilliantly brought out. Greens (as shown by tests with Philips flashbulbs) are better rendered than in sunlight. So there is something to be said for using flashbulbs, in case of need, for photographing spinach.

Colour rendering with flashbulbs, however, depends on the shutter speed used. Using the X contact with small blue flashbulbs and flash cubes at $1/_{50}$ to $1/_{60}$ sec. gives rather bluer results than $1/_{30}$ sec. A particularly warm tone results from the use of $1/_{60}$ sec. (or any slower speed) with the M contact.

The particularly favourable colour rendering with $1/_{60}$ sec. and X contact is doubtless attributable to the fact that the shutter has already closed before the bulb has radiated the last traces of light. Because the blue lacquer covering the bulb becomes scorched during the firing of the bulb the last trace of light is considerably redder than the first radiated. For use as fill light under conditions of exceptionally blue daylight it may however be decidedly advantageous on occasion to make use of the extremely warm residual radiation.

The tendency to blue already mentioned in connection with electronic flash is due to the high content of UV which some flash units radiate, and which is recorded by colour reversal film as a beautiful blue. Apart from this, however, ultra-violet light can also induce fluorescence in all manner of colours, and I have on occasion found that such fluorescence effects can lend quite a striking effect to a picture. An example of this was a stage shot of a New Guinea dancer whose black-and-white check costume came out a bright blue black.

Unfortunately the effect, direct or indirect, of the presence of UV is usually objectionable. It can, however, be completely suppressed by introducing a filter in front of the flash.

Formerly a slightly pink filter was used for this purpose, but it did not prove entirely satisfactory. In particular this type of filter quite appreciably reduces the light intensity. An entirely satisfactory

FILTERS FOR NATURAL COLOUR RENDERING

Light source	Filter
Electronic flash which radiates a great deal of UV	Agfa AK yellow 05 (yellow 10 for stronger effect or Kodak CC 05 Y (CC 10 Y or CC 20 Y for stronger effect) (Use filter in front of flash)
Electronic flash or blue flash bulb with artifical light reversal film	R 12 or 85 B
Clear flashbulbs with daylight reversal film	B 6 or 82 C + 82 A
Clear flashbulbs with artificial light reversal film	R 6 or 81 EF

EQUIPMENT FOR SPECIAL EFFECTS

Purpose	Accessory
Light source filters for pronounced colour effects:	Coloured glasses, transparent coloured paper, coloured foils for theatre lighting
For strobe effects	Photocells

solution is provided by a weak yellow light-balancing gelatine filter. Let us emphasize, however that the filter must be introduced in front of the light source and not the camera lens when you use the flash as fill-in.

One other point must be emphasized here, and that is that many flash units are already provided with a built-in filter. One manufacturer of electronic flash tubes actually uses a yellowish material in the envelopes of the tubes.

The use of yellow filters in this way has yet another advantage: it eliminates possible colour falsification resulting from reciprocity failure due to the short exposure in electronic flash photography (cf. computer flash, page 46). This of course concerns only reversal film, for in the case of negative film any colour cast arising from this cause can be corrected by filtration in the subsequent printing operation. Fluorescence phenomena, when they occur, are not always so easily disposed of, and there is one awkward thing that can happen in photographing architectural interiors: if a photograph is taken by rather weak daylight, requiring an exposure of perhaps 10 to 20 seconds, the long exposure will again introduce reciprocity failure, resulting in a small colour shift. If however relevant parts of the subject are given flash fill light exposures, the short exposure reciprocity failure effect comes in to counteract the first colour shift in those areas. In a colour negative this kind of colour cast compensation is next to impossible to achieve. The only possibility is to use a compensating filter on the electronic flash – always supposing one is lucky enough to know just what colour cast tendencies are present.

Colour cast – or a bogy exposed

Before coming to discuss in detail the composition of a picture with deliberately falsified colour values, I would like just to deal with this matter of colour cast. Personally I have absolutely no respect for it. And the reason is not the fact that I take a whole rucksack full of filters with me wherever I go. Actually this is not necessary. In the first place – as explained in the last section – colour distortion in flash is easily dealt with. Of most importance however is the fact that by use of pictorial composition and in particular by lighting any colour cast can be completely circumvented. However, success in any battle depends upon thoroughly knowing one's enemy. What, then, exactly is colour cast? It is in fact nothing else but a uniform shade of colour which is superimposed over the whole picture, penetrating into its remotest corners.

A green reflection on to a face from, say, a tablecloth may give the picture an unpleasant effect. If the rest of the subject, and particularly the background, appears in normal colours, this still cannot be termed a colour cast.

If on the other hand we use a green ceiling for producing bounce flash, then the whole subject will be steeped in the coloured reflected light from front to back and top to bottom – a true case of colour cast.

But supposing in this flash lighted room with its all-pervading green atmosphere we set a candelabra with candles alight, these will shimmer in quite another colour. Their golden orange tint will stand boldly out against the deep green general lighting.

Again, take the case of a street scene photographed in daylight on artificial light film with the result that the picture is drowned in a heavy blue cast; this can be successfully countered by including in the foreground a red traffic light. The intensity of such a light will dominate any type of colour material.

As an extra a detail could be included in the foreground – say the face of a passer-by – lighted by a clear flash bulb with a yellow filter. Even minute touches of a colour outside the general surrounding hue will work wonders!

Admittedly the colours in question may not correspond to what one is accustomed to regard as ''natural''. It may be an objectively false colour, an exotic colour, an unrealistic, even antirealistic colour, maybe a gaudy, or at the other extreme a symbolically significant colour – whatever kind of colour it may be it still does not come in the category of a colour cast!

Finally two short notes on the subject: False colours do not necessarily add up to a colour cast.

Subjects which are weak in colour, for example, and especially those which are light in tone are extremely sensitive to colour cast. Against white, light yellow, beige, light grey, pale pink and other pastel colours even a quite light, intrinsically unobjectionable colour clash becomes painfully obvious.

Subjects containing much black or very blatant colouring can scarcely be affected by colour casts.

Try it out for yourself: Filter the light used for back, rim, or silhouette lighting of a subject without fill light through bright red, deep blue, citron yellow, bright green or for that matter even lilac filters: the result will certainly be unusual in colour, but there will be no trace of colour cast.

Pictorial composition with highly coloured flash

Large areas of contrasting colour, abruptly confronted, behave like cat and dog – they bite: and the more so the brighter they are.

On the other hand even between blatantly contrasting colours there is never any clash, provided they occur as small touches and fine lines in an otherwise neutral environment, as for instance against a white, grey, or black background.

The practical significance of this bears interesting comparison with the outcome of our investigation into the colour cast problem. A number of differently coloured flashes may without hesitation be used as backlighting so long as there is no fill light. Even a medley of red, green, blue and yellow lines of light are scarcely likely to offend against aesthetic considerations. The black surrounding area softens, harmonizes the harsh conflict of colour. In this "harmonizing" process a really intense colour is in fact closely related to black. I am thinking of blue, and of course especially of dark blue. If I am not mistaken, someone, some time, has already said something culturally significant about this, to the effect that, "Just as yellow always brings with it a luminosity, so can one say that there is always something dark about blue".

And, indeed, that is true. Even if one lights a subject with a subdued blue — maybe even a bluish green — it must still be embellished with spots and lines of red, green, yellow, orange and purple light. This restriction to small touches is all the more important when all or nearly all the colours of the rainbow are used in the lighting.

If — apart from the blue background lighting — only say yellow or red light is used, then it is permissible to add larger areas of coloured light — even maybe the whole foreground subject. A red-blue contrast between foreground and background gives a special "colour perspective" effect. The warm colour shines out aggressively to emphasize the foreground, while the blue background conjures up an impression of space, of distance. Colour photographs of this kind are thus able to achieve a certain three-dimensional effect. And it is here that we come up against a point of discord in the relationship of blue and black. A black background, as opposed to blue, always gives the impression of being nearer. The darkness seems to want to envelop us, to press in and close in upon us. Where the background is illuminated with red, orange, yellow or yellow-green light, it is only within limits that glaring colours can be permitted in the foreground.

In this kind of matter it is always best to try things out for oneself, but there is at any rate one tip which the experimenter can safely follow: There is one kind of foreground which will always give interesting results against any background, irrespective of the colour of the lighting which may be used upon it, and this is the silhouette.

Almost, but not quite so satisfactory as black and blue, as a background to individual coloured light accents, is a white surface. This can be provided either by illuminating a suitable white background with white light or by photographing against the background of a clouded sky.

As filter, almost anything can be placed in front of the light that happens to come handy. I use coloured kite paper or crepe paper, or the transparent coloured foils used for theatrical lighting.

How much light is absorbed by the transparent filters is best ascertained in daylight with an exposure meter, by simply taking a reading on a brightly lighted white surface with and without the filter. This will give at least an approximate guide as to how many stops difference the filter will make to the exposure.

Daylight film and "incorrect" lighting

I find it very satisfactory to use clear flashbulbs (or blue bulbs with the coating removed) with daylight reversal film. They give a pleasantly warm colour rendering. Electronic flash can be made to give a similar rendering by interposing an R 6 filter in front of the reflector. Naturally it is not by any means every situation which will lend itself to an over warm lighting. I have accordingly summarized below the most important situations in which there is nothing against the yellowish-red lighting or which indeed actively demand it.

When, then, should clear flash bulbs or R 6 filtered electronic flash be used?

1 Within the set-up of "colour flash lighting" when yellowish-red is one of the colours desired.

2 To reproduce a warm toned lighting atmosphere such as that of the living room – of table lamps, of illuminated showcases and shop windows, of domestic fires and camp fires. In Chinese lan-

terns or bedside table lamps, as a matter of course I insert clear flash bulbs or warm filtered electronic flash.

3 At night outdoors, where the background is dark. It makes no great difference to the pictorial effect whether the general flash lighting is of the correct colour or is too warm in tone. In the latter case the slightly yellowish-red tint is much more favourable to an impression of street lighting or shop window lighting.

4 On days when the sky is overcast, or in shadow on a sunny day. The warmly lighted foreground provides a pleasant contrast to the cooler toned background. Out of doors, the cool tone of daylight in any case requires appropriate filtering of the warmer toned light of the flash bulb or filtered electronic flash.

5 When there is danger of a blue cast at midday in sunlight. It is true that any such cast can be precisely compensated by an appropriate filter. A warmer tone rendering can however be decidedly better. In particular the brown tones which it imparts to skin are more flattering. I can therefore strongly recommend the use of warm toned lighting on a sunny day at midday.

Artificial light film and "incorrect" lighting

For many flashguns a special warm toned conversion filter is available to adapt them for artificial light, but any R 12 filter will serve (e. g. Wratten 85B). The loss of light in the orange-coloured filter amounts to a good 50 per cent. Clear flashbulbs or blue bulbs with coating removed can be adapted to artificial light film, with only $1/2$ stop light loss, with an R 6 (or Wratten 81 EF) filter. Manipulations of this kind can be necessary when photographic tungsten lamps or spotlights (stage lighting or sports stadia) have to be mixed with flash and for some or other reason excessive importance is attached to absolutely correct colour rendering.

On the other hand flash lighting filtered in this way can also be mixed with daylight. The flash lighted foreground then appears in natural colours on the artificial light film, but the background will be completely blue. The resulting effect can be very attractive.

But are there any occasions when even unfiltered flash lighting can be used with artificial light film?

170

Colour films and flash. A, Daylight reversal film can be used with blue flashbulbs and electronic flash. Clear flashbulbs need filtering. Artificial light film is not intended for flash use. Clear bulbs with a suitable filter can, however, be used. B, Colour negative film can be used with any type of flash but blue bulbs or electronic are preferable.

But of course! Here is an example: Some time ago I had the job of setting up an artificial light studio in a ready-made clothing business. For reasons of space I decided to install a few powerful spotlights and to make use of a mixture of different kinds of fluorescent tubes for shadow relief. However the works manager suddenly came up with the demand that for a slide series the models should pose, not as usual before a white, but against a sky blue background. For the studio director this was child's play: silhouette fashion he simply flooded the background with an electronic flash, and – hey presto – right away he had the most magnificent blue background on his artificial light transparencies.

Coloured strobe effects

Stroboscopes are a kind of flash machine gun! They fire a succession of flashes one after the other at great rapidity. This enables a sharp photographic record to be made of the successive phases of rapid movement. As a rule, the individual phases overlap in the photograph, and therefore cannot easily be clearly separated. The improvised strobe technique which is described below differs from a photograph taken with a stroboscope as normally used for scientific purposes in two important respects:

1 It is far less expensive
2 It enables the individual phases to be individually illuminated in different colours.

To take strobe effect photographs needs at least three electronic flash units and two photocells. In front of each flash unit is a differently coloured filter.
To secure the stroboscopic effect use is made only of the very slight triggering delay which always occurs as the photocell responds to the actuating flash impulse. Consequently electronic flash units of the longer flash duration type cannot be employed for this purpose, for their light output suppresses the dark interval so that the separate flashes become merged into one continuous flash. The essential feature of stroboscopic illumination is that it is intermittent, and the dark interval is vital.

172

Under no circumstances however may the first flash which occurs be permitted to actuate all the remaining cells simultaneously, thereby triggering all the flashes. The flash units must send out their flashes strictly in succession. This is purely a matter of adjusting each individual cell to its respective flash unit. I connect the photocell with its flash unit by an extension cable and set it up directly in front of the other flash unit by which it is to be actuated. Pieces of cardboard are used to screen the photocell from the other flash sources which might otherwise actuate it. So far as the Mecalux is concerned, since this also reacts to reflected light, I cover over the window partly with black adhesive tape to the point where its response sensitivity has been so reduced that it will operate only from the direct flash immediately in front of it. To satisfy myself that the set-up will in fact operate correctly, the flashes occuring one after the other and not simultaneously, I carry out a series of tests, in each of which a different photocell is switched off. The flash unit immediately behind it in the chain, and the following units, should then fail to operate.

Strobe effect photographs must be taken against a completely black background. The flash units can all be set up close one beside the other – and may be used, for example, as back or rim lighting.

Since the flashes in the arrangement described follow one another in very rapid succession, the technique should be used only for recording really rapid movement.

A strobe-related effect can be simply achieved with only two light sources; this consists in photographing a rapid movement with an electronic flash and a flash bulb – suitable filtered in different colours.

The electronic flash records a sharp image, while the flash bulb shows some movement blur.

Special
Techniques

Flash is a versatile form of lighting that can be used on almost any photographic subject. The previous chapters have dealt with the reasonably straightforward techniques. Now we turn to some of the specialised fields in which flash lighting can play an important part.

Close-up and macro photography

In the close-up range it is no longer possible to place implicit reliance on guide numbers and stop tables. In the strictest sense the critical limit lies at about 6½ feet; if we place more reliance on practice than on theory, at 5 feet. So that there may be no misunderstanding, this relates of course not to the camera-subject distance but to the distance between the illuminating flash and the close-up subject.

It stands to reason that even with the camera brought right up close to the subject there is nothing to prevent the flash unit from being taken back, by means of an extension cable, to any distance for which the light output is still adequate. This even has the advantage of providing a very high quality of lighting (tele light). In practice this increase in light distance is admittedly limited to medium close-ups and the use of supplementary lenses. In the case of extreme close-ups or macrophotographs there comes a point when the lighting is inadequate, and the flash must then be brough to within about the same distance as the camera. This is not the place to enlarge upon the subject of how much extra light is required to compensate for camera extension. However it must be remembered that exposure corrections demanded by camera conditions must of course be allowed for in addition to those imposed by the special conditions of close-up lighting which are the subject of the present discussion.

There are three main reasons why corrections have to be made to the guide number:

1 The absence of room reflections inherent in close-up work (page 44). I can only emphasize that this is the most crucial cause. Since it is fundamental for all close-up shots that an allowance has to be made for the fact there is no contribution to exposure

by reflection from the walls, no additional correction has to be made on this score for outdoor shots at night.

2 The fact that the reflector area is quite large in relation to its distance from the subject. The inverse square law is strictly valid only for a point source of light. At great distances all luminous areas are in effect point sources. Conversely on near approach the size of even a small source begins to become important. As the source comes nearer the lighting intensity on the subject no longer increases rapidly in inverse proportion to the square of the distance – or, as here, the square of its proximity to the subject. Because an ever increasing number of rays from the edge of the reflector no longer hit the subject, but pass it by, the growth of the lighting intensity slows up. As many modern flash units have small reflectors, the effect just described is of less importance than the absence of room reflection.

3 Parallax. When the flash unit is mounted in the accessory shoe of the camera, the illuminating beam remains parallel to the camera axis. As the camera is brought closer to the subject, more of the flash rays bypass the subject until, at very close range, only those from the edge of the reflector nearest to the subject actually reach it. Something has to be done about this. The flash can be aimed directly at the centre of the subject by means of a tilting device in the accessory shoe or a flash bracket. In extreme close-up the fixed flash in the accessory shoe provides side lighting, sometimes even rim lighting. At such close quarters frontal lighting is achievable only with a ring flash attachment.

The somewhat uncertain exposure conditions of close-up photography naturally invite the recommendation that the photographer should arrive at the correct exposure by way of preliminary tests. When, therefore, I give recommendations by way of a general guide, I would suggest that occasional tests be made, on a not too difficult subject, so as to have a safe procedure cut and dried in emergency. That is not to say that tests should be made every millimetre over the whole 10–100 cm range: the best way is to decide once and for all on two or three standard flash distances, preferably such as will in emergency allow the flash to remain on the camera. It is a good plan to provide a flash bracket which can be swung forward and backward so that the camera can be moved a certain amount towards or away from the subject while maintaining the flash-subject distance constant. For my own flash unit I have made a cord with knots at 4, 12 and 24 inch distances. Thus I can measure the distances in a twinkling for which actual tests have previously been made.

Here then is the table! But once again I would like to emphasize that these recommendations should only be followed as a guide. I hope anyway that they will in practice prove reliable to within not much more than half a stop up or down, but they are subject, of course to the usual adjustments for rim lighting, back lighting, etc., and for increased extension.

EXPOSURE GUIDE FOR CLOSE-UPS

Flash-subject distance	for electronic flash (fully charged)	for flash bulbs (or for electronic flash units immediately after the neon pilot lamp has lit up)
4–5 feet	expose according to guide number	calculate exposure from guide number but open up lens a further $1/2$ stop
2–4 feet	calculate exposure from guide number but open up lens a further $1/2$ to 1 stop	calculate exposure from guide number but open up lens a further 1 to $1^1/2$ stops
less than 2 feet	calculate exposure from guide number but open up lens a further $1^1/2$ stops	halve the guide number and expose accordingly

Automatic flash units for the most part can be used quite satisfactorily right into the close-up region. According to the manufacturers' official statements they function down to a working distance of 2 feet: unofficially they are claimed to operate at half that distance. If there is a great deal of dark background, or open space which is reproduced as dark, the sensor can of course give misleading readings. If the subject occupies only a very small part of the picture, the diaphragm should be closed down a further 1 to $1^1/2$ stops.

178

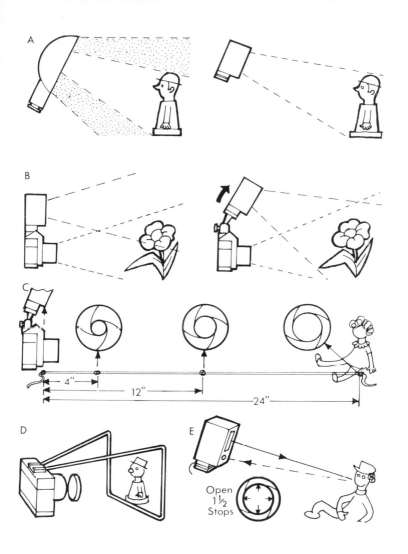

Flash problems. A, As large reflector approaches closer, inverse square law fails. Smaller units are less affected. B, In close-ups, flash on camera may need tilting. C, Measuring card for close-ups at predetermined distances and apertures. D, Frame for fixed distance close-up. E, Automatic units may call for diaphragm adjustment in close-ups.

179

The ring flash

A ring flash is an electronic flash tube in ring form which can be operated from a number of different electronic flash units. As the name implies, these are annular – ring-shaped – electronic flash tubes mounted in ring-shaped reflectors. The resulting unit is placed like a collar around the camera lens. The respective manufacturers are always pleased to provide information on the adapters necessary to fit them to particular lenses. Understandably the ring flash eliminates any kind of shadow formation. These special light sources are primarily designed for general close-up work, but in particular they are of great value in medical photography: where the subject of the photograph is deep down in a narrow cavity the luminous collar as a rule affords the only possible means of lighting it. I regard the ring flash as a most useful accessory not only in close-up work, but also quite generally where a uniform flood of frontal light is need. I do not myself possess a ring flash, but notwithstanding my predilection for solo flash, on occasion I have to resort to the use of a number of flash units and if need be – especially when photographing insects – I mount up four small flash units in a kind of ring flash formation. A Mecablitz S 16 is mounted in the camera accessory shoe. With the help of two flash brackets two further units are attached, one beneath the camera body and one each to right and left. The S 16 above the camera is operated by the centre contact. Its reflected light triggers the other three, all of which are connected to a Mecalux triggering unit. This may sound a lot of heavy clutter around the camera. In fact, the flash units are so light that all four are no great weight. The lighting effect in the close-up region resulting from the light which emanates from the group of flash units may not perhaps be quite equal to that of a ring flash, but it comes very close to it.

While ring flash, and substitute equipment, obviates cast shadows, at the same time it gives rise to quite considerable reflection effects by virtue of its frontal character. Attempts have been made to eliminate this by the use of polarized light.

In this way reflections which otherwise would inevitable mar photographs of medical and biological specimens, or plants, and of oil paintings, are amazingly suppressed. Extinction of reflec-

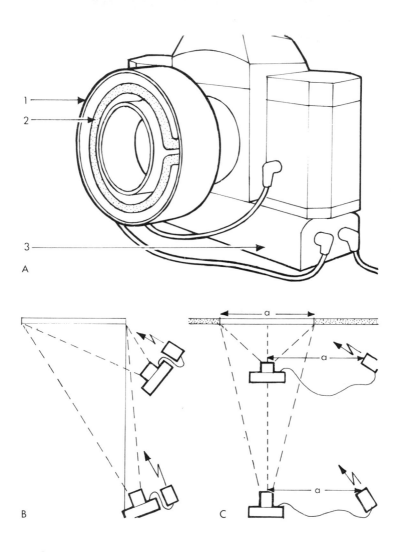

Special applications. A, Ring flash for shadowless lighting in close ups. 1, Reflector. 2, Circular flash cube. 3, Power pack. B, Shooting through glass. With a wide-angle lens the angle must be oblique. The long-focus lens can shoot straighter. C, Through window with flash off camera. With camera used head on, flash must be displaced from lens axis by distance equal to window width. Long-focus lens allows less acute angle.

tions from glass surfaces is not perfect, those from metal still less so.

As a rough and ready rule: Reflections which merely cause the specimen to glisten can be quite well eliminated by a polarizing ring flash. Wherever bright reflections occur, at best some degree of suppression may be expected. Images of the light source then appear deep blue. The device devours – one can no longer speak merely of absorbing – light to the equivalent of three stops! From the point of view of brightness its only value is for close-up work, but in this field its performance is fantastic.

Flash through glass: aquaria and shop windows

Luck and glass are both said to be fragile: When glass is involved – or more precisely the reflections which it causes – luck in flash photography can go to the pieces. Nevertheless a pane of glass should give no cause for anxiety. It is easy enough to penetrate the glass windows of aquaria, and terraria, showcases and shop windows, with flash. And here is the secret of how to beat the reflections – instead of having them beat you.

Let us assume that only one camera is available, with built-in or slip-on flash unit. On no account may the flash be directed straight at the glass from the front. This could only result in one gigantic reflection. The flash must be aimed, and the photograph taken, obliquely through the pane. This procedure is not very satisfactory, on account of both lack of sharpness and colour fringes which are likely to result. But beggars can't be choosers! One sure way of obviating reflections is to photograph through the glass at such an angle that no part of it is perpendicular to the camera axis. The longer the focal length of the camera lens, the easier this is to achieve. The diagram shows this quite clearly. If a wide angle lens is used the angle of view must be very obliquely inclined to the glass surface. A very long focus lens enables the lens to be directed almost, though not quite, perpendicularly to the surface.

Something, too, can be achieved by juggling with the format – where this is not square. In the case of a horizontal format the camera is just displaced upwards or downwards, with vertical formats to right or left. Needless to say I also turn the camera round so that the flash is on the left hand side when I am photographing the window from the left, and vice versa.

Incidentally, even if the flash is taken off the camera and moved to one side so that the camera can be used square on to the window, this is considerably easier to carry out if a long focus lens is used.

To ensure freedom from reflection, the flash unit must be displaced to the left or right, or up or down as the case may be, by a distance at least as great as the width, or height, of the section of window embraced by the viewfinder.

Sometimes one hears the – somewhat ambiguous – recommendation to place the light source right up against the glass to avoid reflections. However the lighting that results is very hard.

Aquarium and terrarium photographs in particular lend themselves quite well to the use of a second, fill light. As the type of fill lighting normally used – frontal or bounce lighting – is unfortunately inadmissible in this case, the second light source, which should if possible be weaker (distance $1/4$ greater), should be directed so obliquely from the side or from above that there is no possibility of the formation of double shadows. In the case of water filled containers the risk of any conspicuous double shadow formation is fortunately not very great. Care must however be taken – using for instance a dark piece of cardboard – to screen any direct light from reaching the camera. If this should become reasonably well illuminated, its image will appear reflected in the window, with most objectionable effect. If necessary, camera and tripod must be covered in black paper.

Finally a few notes relating to exposure, with special reference to aquarium photography but – with the exception of the last point – applicable to other work involving illumination through a window.

There is a loss of light resulting from the following causes:

1 The absence of room reflection – particularly when the walls of the aquarium are dark – represents a light loss equivalent to $1/2$ stop (electronic flash) to 1 stop (small flashbulbs).

2 There is a loss by reflection at all air-glass and glass-water surfaces. Any light which is thus scattered by reflection is lost so far

as the subject is concerned. The proportion of light thus lost will depend upon the angle at which it strikes the surface. The more oblique this angle the greater the proportion lost. If the angle between the incident light beam and the glass surface is greater than 40°, the slight loss of light need not be taken into account. At 40° however there is a light loss equivalent to $1/4$ stop, at 20 to 25° $1/2$ stop, at 15° 1 stop, and at the extremely oblique angle of 10° more than 2 stops. This should be reason enough so far as possible to avoid the use of wide angle lenses for through-the-window photography, since of necessity they demand the use of very oblique lighting.

3 The water of an aquarium also absorbs light. How much is lost from this cause depends on the one hand on the turbidity of the water itself, and on the other the thickness of the layer of water which has to be penetrated. However, since fish are usually photographed while they are close to the window the loss of light from this cause is as a rule not more than the equivalent of about $1/2$ stop.

Taking all factors into account we arrive at an average guide number correction of $1 1/2$ to 2 stops. Where the wails are light and the light source is at a considerable distance a correction of about 1 stop should suffice.

Flash under water

At first glance it is impossible to tell from an underwater photograph whether it was taken by a diver with full compressed air diving equipment at 130 feet depth or by a snorkel swimmer a couple of inches beneath the surface.

Most underwater photographs, irrespective of the depth at which they were taken, owe their existence to flash – and more especially to the small flashbulb.

Water acts like a blue filter; at close-up range the warm light of the small blue flashbulb gives the picture a pleasant tone. At distances above 3 feet clear bulbs give better results. The extreme limit of distance for blue bulbs is about 6–7 feet. The flash duration of these bulbs – $1/80$ to $1/100$ sec. – is rather long to catch a clear picture of fish in motion, especially if they should happen to be in a bit of a hurry. The glittering fish scales reflect flash extraordinarily powerfully, and this means that the "tailing off" of the flash (page 59) becomes still more evident in prolonging the exposure. With $1/30$ sec. and the X contact, at very shallow depths daylight still has considerable effect on the film. The result is a warm toned, perhaps half sharp flash image superimposed on a completely blue daylight image. However attractive "mixed" images of this kind may be in other fields, pictures of fish should always be dead sharp.

Fortunately small flashbulbs can also be used with $1/60$ sec. on the X contact, losing only the equivalent of $1/2$ stop in light. The faster shutter speed quite considerably reduces the danger of an unsharp subsidiary image. The fraction of the flash duration actually utilized amounts to only about $1/200$ sec. What is important, however, is that the early closing of the shutter cuts out the "luminous tail". The bright reflections on the fish cannot then act on the film for longer than the bare $1/200$ sec. Underwater photographers who use between-lens shutters can well avail themselves of the M contact with $1/125$ or $1/150$ sec. Suitable flashbulbs for this purpose are the PF 5, No. 5, or Press 25. Admittedly there may not be much future in this, for who knows how long the M contact will continue to be provided in shutters?

Close-ups offer the best chance of success in underwater photography. The (apparent) subject distance of 6–7 feet may not be the absolute limit for underwater flash photography, but in general there is not much point in greatly exceeding it. At greater distances the subject assumes a heavy blue cast irrespective of the flash. In addition, the minute particles in the water, just as happens with tobacco smoke in a smoke-filled room, create troublesome scattering of light (page 78). The thicker the layer of water between subject and light source, the more apparent is the effect. One quite useful expedient in ameliorating this effect would be the use of back lighting. Unfortunately this is scarcely practicable under water. If ever there was a clear case for keeping the flash on the camera for reasons of operating convenience, it must be in swimming and diving. The worst effects of scatter are encountered with frontal lighting. It is therefore advisable to make the bracket carrying the flash unit of considerable length – about

20 inches. It should also be so constructed that it can be swung forward so that the flash is directed straight at the subject. In this way, at least in close-up, a pronounced side or top lighting can be achieved which minimizes the effects of scatter and also contributes to a three-dimensional effect.

There can be no harm in using a second light as fill light, especially if there is not much daylight. This second light should be as close as possible to the camera body, so that it illuminates the subject as nearly as possible from directly in front. Its light output can be reduced either by removing the reflector or by partially blacking it over.

Determination of flash exposure is a thing quite on its own. On the one hand, under water there is usually no shadow filling reflected light; on the other hand, water heavily absorbs and scatters light, so that only a fraction of the light emitted by the flash unit reaches the subject. The amount of this wastage depends upon the turbidity of the water.

If the turbidity is very pronounced there is absolutely no purpose in attempting to use flash. If the water is clear, the first tests should be based on the following rule of thumb, which is valid for (apparent) distances up to $6^1/2$ feet:

$$f = \frac{L}{3 \cdot a_s}$$

where f = required stop, L = normal guide number for a particular flash unit used with a particular film, and a_s = apparent distance in feet

Thus we divide the normal guide number by 3, which gives our new special underwater guide number. This must then be divided by – not the true distance – but the apparent, shorter distance. Because of the refraction of the water, fish, seaweed, rocks – everything we see – appears to be about $1/4$ nearer than it actually is. Thus a fish 6 feet away appears to be only $4^1/2$ feet off. If the seabed appears to be 10 feet down beneath us, it is really just over 13 feet away.

The rule is therefore: Multiply the apparent distance by 1.33 to obtain the actual distance.

All this may sound very confusing, but in fact it need hardly bother us at all, for the reflex finder, the camera, and our eyes are all equally deceived. All we have to do is to pretend that the apparent distance is the real distance.

But remember: our golden underwater formula for flash exposure is after all only a guide, and not every eye will find it equally accurate. There can be no substitute for actual tests.

Underwater flash photography can be great fun – provided the flashbulbs fire! The contacts of the bulb holder, like the bulbs themselves, are freely exposed to the water. Consequently oxidation of leads and contacts must inevitably sooner or later cause an ignition failure. The best remedy is to coax an accommodating member of the household to make a habit of giving a real good clean-up to all exposed contacts before all snorkel expeditions.

Photographing birds in rapid flight

Basically, it is useless to attempt to stalk a bird with the camera. The probability – to be optimistic – of getting a reasonably sharp picture is of the order of one in a million. There remains only a chance that some spot can be found to which the bird has periodically to return, and on which we can keep our camera trained in the hope of snapping it. (Such a spot might be a bird house in winter.) There is only one place to which a bird is absolutely certain to return, however, and that is its nest.

During the spring a pair of birds had carelessly built their nest right in front of the door leading from my room into the garden. It was in the fork of a cherry tree, about 7 1/2 feet above the ground. Soon a nestling hatched out. My ambitions were aroused. I wanted to get a picture of the baby with its mother. One thing was clear: I must make my photographic preparations so carefully that the birds were not frightened off. If by fussing around I were to drive off the parents, the baby bird would be left to starve, and I wasn't going to risk that. For days on end, therefore, I left the garden door slightly open, and behind the slit I set up my tripod with the Leica and the 400 mm Telyt. (This was my first attempt at bird photography. Later I found that the 90 mm lens was quite adequate.)

The birds became accustomed to the open door and the comic looking tripod behind it. On the left beside the door I fixed up a flashgun about 6 feet distant and 10 feet above the ground, so that it was above the nest and could shine down into it. The flash was connected to the camera by an extension lead. The nest was completely in the shade, and even with a 400 ASA film, without the flash full aperture would have been necessary.

Many nature photographers have established the fact that most living creatures are not specially bothered by flash: after all, they are quite used to thunderstorms. The brief flash is in fact far less disturbing to them than a flash of sunshine directed into the nest by a mirror or a piece of polished metal.

The camera was set up rather below the level of the nest.

The little bird could only be seen and photographed when it stretched its neck right out, which it did only when one of its parents flew in with food in its beak. This is what always happened: One of the parent birds suddenly appeared. The youngster piped up noisily. The parent hesitated, deposited its booty in the youngster's beak, immediately took some rubbish from the nest into its crop and flew off. The whole procedure as a rule occupied only five or six seconds, and that was all the time I had to make the exposure, after which I had to lie in wait once more for 5 to 30 minutes. The approach of either of the birds was always quite sudden, without any warning. I observed that the bird never flew direct to the nest, but first alighted, for example, on the nearby roof, and from there flew a zigzag course to the nest.

On the second day, it was almost exclusively the mother bird that came to the nest. I was finding the waiting behind the camera too long, so every time the mother left the nest I returned to my desk to work. Between the feeds I should always have quite a long interval – or so at least I thought. But then the bird started appearing suddenly at very short intervals. The enthusiastic cheeping of the baby bird was very plainly to be heard. I decided to make the following experiment: If I waited behind the camera the bird appeared about every 20 minutes, but if I went away to my desk it came every five minutes. It was clear then that despite my precautions the bird was still somewhat disturbed. How did it know whether I was behind my desk or just behind the door? Quite by chance I hit upon the secret! On one side of my house is a window. Before returning to the nest the clever bird flew past this window, and through it satisfied itself as to where I was sitting.

On the strength of this, in order to get as many shots in as possible, after each shot I settled down behind the desk and waited there until the bird again flew past the window. As it still had a few camouflage flights to make before returning to the nest I just had time to get back to the camera. In this way I could take pictures every five minutes – at least for the next four flights! After which I again had to wait in patience. I sat at the desk – and no bird came past. The cheeping of the young bird however told me that the mother must have visited the nest a number of times without my having the opportunity of returning quickly to the camera. The solution to the puzzle? Before flying back to the nest the bird proceeded on foot past my door and made sure by looking through the slit where I was hiding!

Some readers may find this story a bit hard to believe. But I can assure them that I am prepared to vouch for it. I personally feel that at least the earlier investigators into animal behaviour underestimated the intelligence of many animals and perhaps overestimated human intelligence. On the evening of the second day I developed my pictures. Despite the wide aperture, even the night pictures were sharp. Characteristically the daylight shots gave a better rendering of the atmosphere, while the flash photographs revealed far more biological details.

Flash technique in copying

I was once asked to photograph some relatively small paintings hung quite high on a wall, close, in fact, to the ceiling. Unless a long focus lens were used the pictures would inevitably have come out extremely distorted. A long focus lens on the other hand can record such high placed subjects *almost* – theoretically speaking – and in practice completely as though they were at ground level. This is due to the fact that when photographing from a long distance the camera axis is *almost* perpendicular even to a high placed subject.

Let us suppose that the picture, about 6½ feet wide, is hanging high up on the wall, the centre of the picture being 13½ feet above the camera (tripod height 6½ feet, height of picture above floor 20 feet). With the 9 cm portrait lens it would have to be photographed from about 20 feet to fill the format. The camera axis would then be far from perpendicular to the picture – in point of fact about 40° from vertical. This is a considerable tilt. With the 40 cm Telyt on the Leica a format filling image called for a distance of about 93 feet. From this distance the camera axis deviated only about 7.5° from the perpendicular to the picture surface. This can be taken as acceptable.

However, in order to reduce the tilt to such an amount that the absolute minimum of correction in enlarging would ensure complete freedom from converging verticals, I resorted to yet another little trick. Instead of attempting to make the picture fill the format I increased the distance still further by about 50 per cent. At this, the picture still filled two thirds of the width of the format, while the increase distance brought the camera axis still closer to the perpendicular. But in addition – and this was important – it enabled me to bring the camera axis still closer to the perpendicular by allowing the image of the picture to occupy the upper two thirds of the format instead of being central. All in all this meant that there was as good as no tilt left.

Unfortunately the daylight which fell on the picture from above gave extremely bad lighting. The upper edge of the picture lay in deep shadow, then came an extremely bright band of light. The lower half of the picture was somewhat darker. This is where only flash could help. I used two Philips PF 5 flashbulbs both on the same side below at floor level. I connected several extension cables together so that I could bring the flashguns nearer to the pictures. Ultimately the flash/subject distance was brought to about 50 feet. The lens was used at f4.8, its full aperture.

Now it may well be asked whether lighting of this kind, which illuminates the subject from one side only, can give uniform illumination. However the uniformity of illumination is basically better the farther the light source is from the subject. I make many copies by flash, using only one light source to one side of the original.

The one proviso here is that the flash is used as a tele light. I use a 13.5 cm lens, keeping the flash at about the same distance as the camera, with the result that, at this ratio of picture size to distance, the lighting is always uniform. In the example quoted, according to my calculation the 6$\frac{1}{2}$ foot picture was so uniformly lighted that the lower edge received only about 5 per cent more light than the top edge. It is impossible to detect this in the photograph. And if I should have only one flashgun available, limiting me to a flash distance of 40 feet, the fall-off in illumination intensity would at most be 11 per cent, which is of no account in practice. And as already explained, these values can be still further improved by aiming the light not at the centre of the subject but at the upper edge. The lower edge of the picture, being somewhat nearer the light source, receives light from the side of the reflector. The upper, more distant edge is more powerfully illuminated by light around the axis of the reflector. In practice, it is true, it is often neither possible nor justifiable to calculate everything so accurately.

To take a practical example, let us assume that the light source is used at the considerable obliquity of 45° between lighting and camera axis, and is directed precisely at the farther corner of the subject. If the flash/subject distance is three times the width of the subject, there will be an alarmingly high lighting contrast of 1 : 2. If instead we choose a flash distance of ten times the subject width this contrast shrinks to the quite insignificant value of 1 : 1.18. At 15 times distance it shrinks even further to 1 : 1.12.

Incidentally I would like once again to point out that the obliquity of lighting of 45° between camera axis and lighting axis in copying, in contrast to ordinary subjects having spatial depth, requires a half stop wider aperture than "normal". 60° requires 1 stop, 70° requires 2, and 75° three stops aperture increase. However, so oblique a lighting is normally not used for flat copy. A long light source/subject distance – and this is not restricted to the photography of paintings – does not permit reflections from glossy surfaces even though they may not for some reason have been suppressed by use of our aquarium rule.

At Aiyion in the Gulf of Corinth I once had to photograph an ikon which was completely encased in embossed silver sheet and further protected above by glass. Flash, used close up, gave rise to a regular firework display of reflections from the precious metal relief. From the greatest possible distance permitted by the chapel I directed a PF 60 B slightly sideways onto the ikon.

Reflections, basically, are nothing more or less than images of a light source. In consequence of the considerable distance the image formed by the reflector of the silver surface is so small that the minute highlights just could not interfere with the general impression.

It was a much simpler matter to photograph late Byzantine wall frescoes in the Palaiachora on Aiyion. In the little 13th to 14th century church the lighting was fairly dim, but uniform. Using a tripod, I first took black-and-white photographs. Exposures under the most favourable conditions were about 5 seconds – at worst, about 30 seconds.

However, I gave special care to colour photography on colour reversal material. In order to arrive at an exact comparison I shot first of all a long time exposure without flash, and then a further one with a PF 1 B used as tele light. The transparency taken without flash exhibited the characteristic colour cast due to reciprocity failure. The flash shot reproduced the colours true to nature and delicately graded.

Improvised back projection

Back projection can be improvised with a simple slide projector with its projection lamp replaced by a Type 5 flashbulb (the built in heat absorbing filter should be removed). If possible a flash gun with the reflector removed should be inserted from above into the slide projector. The flash is then synchronized with the camera. The greatest care must be taken that the flash bulb is actually located just where the filament of the projection lamp is normally situated. Needless to say, for flash projection even projectors whose normal performance leaves much to be desired will suffice.

Before actually making the flash exposure, the transparency should be projected in the ordinary way with the projector lamp. This is important both for focusing and for exposure tests. The stop required for photographing the projected image can be determined by measurement once a conversion factor has been established by means of a test series.

My procedure is as follows: First of all I make a trial exposure on the back projection with the normal projection lamp, following exactly the indication of the exposure meter. Suppose the result gave 1 second at f5.6. I then make a series of flash tests with apertures from f2.8 to f11.

Let us suppose that the result given by the f8 test corresponded to the projection lamp picture. From this it follows that to obtain the same result at f8 with the projection lamp as with the flash an exposure of 2 seconds must be given. This gives the required conversion factor. I simply set the exposure meter to 2 seconds, and the reading which I obtain on the projected image will be correct for the flash exposure. The most widely used professional flash system uses front projection; for our purposes translucent screen back projection is considerably more satisfactory. Front projection inevitably calls for oblique shooting, and in my experience this entails a whole crowd of difficulties. As projection screen I have quite successfully used translucent paper. Admittedly the projection lens is sometimes seen shining through, and it is then of course essential that this "hot spot" as it is termed, should be covered with the foreground subject.

If the main subject is left unlighted, it appears as a silhouette, and this can give quite interesting effects. Otherwise the lighting of the subject must be so arranged that no direct light, and as little as possible scattered light, reaches the screen. This involves, among others, the following precautions:

1 Use side, rim, back, or top lighting. Avoid front lighting.
2 Screen the light source itself from the projection screen with dark cardboard. If the room has light walls which might reflect light on to the screen, cover them over.
3 For subject lighting, if possible use electronic flash because its illuminating angle is quite small.
4 To assist in eliminating room reflections use close-up lighting.

It need scarcely be emphasized that the arrangement and intensity of the subject lighting must be tailored to the stop demanded by the backprojected image.

A picture of this kind gains greatly in realism by logical and systematic lighting. The direction of the subject lighting must harmonize with the direction from which the light would appear to be coming in the projected picture.

Whether or not the final result succeeds in maintaining the illusion of reality depends on the arrangement of the foreground subject. Nowhere should it be possible to detect the transition between it and the projected background. Models who have to appear in toto right down to the soles of their feet should stand on a slight elevation of the ground – a mound of sand, a piece of rock, a felled tree trunk – which cuts across the bottom of the projection screen. Still better is some sturdy object such as a boat, or a fence, which can be used as a support for the model. The most convincing pictures are those incorporating in the foreground some form of vista – through branches, archways, a window etc. This enhances the three-dimensional illusion.

Flash photography by reflected UV

Daylight – and electronic flash – both contain a considerable proportion of invisible ultra-violet radiation. Films are sensitive to UV. Colour films record it as blue. The glass of photographic lenses is transparent to long wave UV. The only additional accessory needed is a black filter which absorbs visible light but transmits the UV.

The special characteristic of UV reflection photography lies in the fact that the subject is reproduced in unusual, often surprising tones. Interesting results may be expected at the first attempt from photographs of flowers. But in fact the peculiar potentialities of UV reflection photography are put to valuable use in botanical and zoological, and also in criminological investigations. UV filters, not UV-absorbing filters, are available for this type of photography from various manufacturers. Generally, they call for an exposure increase of about 5 or 6 stops.

To record the UV radiation – with as little as possible visible light – reflected from the subject, all that is necessary is to place the filter on the lens. As the focal length of the camera lens for UV is somewhat shorter than for visible light, it is advisable to set the focus for slightly longer than the actual distance of the subject. If the subject is 10 feet away, the distance scale should be set to, say, 13 feet.

When using a reflex camera I focus the subject through a deep blue filter.

The infra-red dark flash

To take photographs by ultra-violet radiation in total darkness is practically impossible. It is in the highest degree probable that the UV will encounter materials which fluoresce under its influence and so insidiously betray the photographer. Small wonder, then, that whenever it comes to photographing in the dark, it is infra red film that steps into the breach.

However, while the UV photograph must be regarded as a speciality of electronic flash, on the IR sector impressive intensities can be achieved with small flash bulbs. On the other hand, electronic flash is perfectly capable of producing IR photographs.

The accompanying table sets out some IR flash guide numbers which have the virture of having been actually tried out. They are based on the use of a gelatine IR black filter (Kodak Wratten No. 87). To ensure that the flash unit is so sealed that no trace of visible light can escape, it can, for example, be enclosed in a small cardboard box. This is of course provided with an "infra-red window" consisting of Wratten gelatine No. 87 filter. However no matter how carefully such a light-tight box is constructed, a very faint, scarcely perceptible red shimmer of light still penetrates the filter. On occasion I suppress even this to the point of invisibility with a piece of tissue paper inserted beneath the filter.

The infra-red colour film mentioned in the table records visible light (green, yellow, and red) on two of its coatings, while the third coating gives a completely red dark flash picture. If visible light is present, this records, depending upon the filter used on the camera lens, bluish, greenish, or whitish.

GUIDE NUMBERS FOR INFRA-RED FILM

Type of film	IR flash guide number for X contact, $1/30$ sec. Wratten 87 filter	
	PF 1 B M 2 B, AG 3 B	PF 5 B, No. 58 Press 25 B
Kodak IR 135	33	50
Kodak Aero Ektachrome Infrared	59	98

Details of infra-red technique, such as the lengthening of camera extension, naturally apply equally to dark flash photography.

Special tricks with photocells

Photocells respond well to infra-red radiation. This has potentialities for all sorts of tricks.

Take the case in which it is desired to trigger flash back lighting without using a cable but without the slave actuating flash being apparent. All that is necessary is to attach an IR black filter to the triggering flash unit on the camera, thereby suppressing the visible component of the flash.

Some types of photocell respond not simply to a high light intensity, but to a sudden rise in intensity. If a spotlight is shone continuously on them nothing happens. But if the light is switched off and then, after a brief interval, on again, the sudden illumination will cause it to trigger a flash unit connected to it.

I have used this effect to produce "chain reaction" pictures. Thus not long ago I took a triple strobe photograph of a tennis ball on its rebound from the racket. This involved triggering the first flash very precisely at the instant when the ball had moved only a few millimetres after being hit. With rapid movement of this order there would not be a chance in a thousand of achieving the required accuracy with an ordinary manual release. I therefore employed the open flash method in a darkened room as follows: The ball was suspended on a thread from the ceiling, and a projector focused on it. In the shadow of the ball was placed the photocell of a slave unit. As the ball was hit and moved from its position shielding the photocell, the light from the projector struck the photocell which in turn, $1/1600$ sec. later triggered the flash. In this way I "strobe-flashed" 12 exposures one after another with such accuracy that no single picture was to early or too late by a fraction of a $1/100$ sec.

One problem which this presented was of course the projector beam, which during the time the shutter was open would have completely overexposed the ball. To obviate this I inserted a dark red filter in the gate of the projector. (I had of course previously removed the cold light filter from the projector.) This provided a complete solution.

Such tricks are like sand on the sea shore! Here, in brief, are a few of them:

Behind a pile of bricks a slave photocell is set up in the shadow of one particular brick. If the whole pile is made to collapse, the flash will fire at the instant this block becomes displaced.

I had hoped that it would be possible to trigger a slave unit with a falling body. To check this, I once again used the trick of training a projector beam on the photocell, and then releasing the ball in such a way that in its fall its shadow interrupted the light beam. The result was negative! Nothing happened! If I held my hand for only a few seconds in front of the cell and then removed it, it promptly reacted.

It would seem that the device is dazzled by bright light and needs 5 to 6 seconds to recover. The falling ball would be a case for the light barrier technique. In contrast to the strobe technique this responds not to the removal of an obstruction to a light beam, but to the opposite – the breaking of the beam by an obstruction.

Recently it has become possible to connect battery operated electric remote releases direct to photocell slave units. (I have myself tested out, for this purpose, a combination of the Metz Mecalux and the Schiansky Teleknips 601.)

Special effects with focal plane shutters

If an electronic flash unit is attached to the X contact of some cameras with a focal plane shutter set to $1/125$ sec., the flash will illuminate only about $1/3$ of the format. If a photograph is taken under these conditions in daylight, the whole picture will be exposed in the ordinary way to the daylight illumination, but only part of it to the flash lighting.

I have found this useful for making demonstration photographs for lecture purposes, showing, for example, in a single photograph how differently a face can appear with and without fill lighting.

On the other hand a flashbulb can be used to give silhouette lighting over the whole background. If electronic flash is used as fill light, of two figures in the foreground one will appear only in outline, the other with detail revealing fill light.

It is, I must admit, not all that easy to ensure that the dividing line between illuminated and unilluminated zones comes just where it is wanted. Subjects which admit of rather more tolerance in this respect are much more likely to turn out successfully than those which call for meticulous accuracy.

It is convenient to reproduce a subject in the unilluminated section of the picture and in the illuminated section its image in a mirror. The artificial light film method (page 170) brings out the effect particularly clearly.

What shutter speed to use, and which will be the bigger section to light, can be determined by the enlarging paper method (page 30).

High-output bulbs and triggering equipment

Extremely high output flashbulbs are occasionally needed for reportage, fashion, advertising and stage photography and especially for interior and exterior architectural photography.

These comprise – according to needs – clear or blue flashbulbs with standard screw sockets. Like the small flashbulbs, these are operated on voltages from 3 to 30 V. Mains operation, with most types, is inadmissible, unless 8 bulbs are connected in series on 220 volts (4 on 110 volts) for use on open flash, or alternatively a series resistor of 40 to 60 ohms is used.

The output of the clear flashbulbs – and in this they differ from the small bulbs – is about double that of the blue bulbs. The combination of artificial light film, clear flashbulb, and R 6 (or Wratten 81 C) filter, as compared with a daylight film of equal speed and blue flashbulb, gives a gain in effective speed of around $2/3$ stop. The whole output of the Philips PF 100, GE No. 50, Sylvania Type 3 (exceptionally only at $1/15$ sec., X contact) is fully utilized. The amount of light lost at $1/30$ sec. (M) may be disregarded, and at $1/60$ (M) – the fastest possible shutter speed – amounts to $1/2$ stop. The $1/3$ or so less powerful PF 60, No. 22, Type 2, are more adaptable, and can even be used with $1/500$ sec. (M contact). This, admittedly, means a loss of light of more than four stops.

It is necessary to distinguish between normal flash guns and ignition, or triggering equipment with safety plug and socket connection for tungsten type photographic lamps with flashbulbs substituted for the tungsten lamps. For some time I worked with the Kobold BC unit, which is equipped for the attachment of five

198

extension flash heads. There is nothing against using the main unit on its own! However if the auxiliary flash heads are left connected up, any residual charge in the capacitor may result in the firing of a bulb on insertion.

The Rolleimarin underwater flash unit can also be used on dry land. It consists of a power pack no bigger than a cigarette box, fitted with a synchronizing cable, to which up to three flash heads can be attached. It is also provided with a socket into which any standard plug can be fitted, and with the addition of a standard three way adapter up to three photographic or other lamps can be connected. These are then fitted with flash bulbs in place of their filament lamps. Using a number of screen lampholders or sockets, to which further flash heads are attached, it is even possible to operate up to 15 flash bulbs from this Rollei power pack. Three groups each of five flash bulbs connected in series are wired in parallel. Alternatively any other capacitor flash unit having a 22.5 volt battery and a 100μF capacitor can be used as the main unit or "power pack". The circuit of linked-up lampholders or sockets have then only to be fitted with a test lamp adapter which in turn is inserted into the socket on the flash unit on the camera. Any sockets in the series circuit which are not in use must of course be short-circuited. I should however say that for myself I prefer ready made triggering equipment to home made "hook-ups". More especially, while series operation of flashbulbs certainly works, it is not absolutely reliable. One or other of the bulbs may fail to ignite.

Flash bulbs which thus fail to ignite should in future be reserved for "solo" use. They are pretty certain to fail again if used in another series circuit. In any case make a practice always of brushing the cap contact of a screw cap bulb against the sole of a shoe before inserting it in order to reduce resistance due to oxidation of the surface by previous use.

Among other equipment suitable for multiple lighting, the Bowen Synchron Six deserves a special note in that its control box has special connections for up to six flash heads but it is still adequately "portable", in the literal sense, as press equipment. At the same time the equipment is adequate for studio use, and, up to a point, for interior architectural photography.

Incidentally the guide numbers quoted for the large flashbulbs incorporate a reflector amplification factor of 4 (or 5 in the case of American models). In point of fact, not all the reflectors primarily designed for photographic lamps provide this degree of amplification.

The best way of checking this is as follows: A 250 watt unsilvered photographic lamp is used to light a test subject first with and then without the reflector. The difference in illuminating power is measured with an exposure meter. If this difference does not prove to be exactly 2 stops, the amplification factor cannot be 4. This test cannot give precise results unless, for the elimination of stray light, it is carried out in a large room or out of doors at night. The distance from light source to subject must be 20 times the diameter of the reflector.

In the case of such deviation from the standard amplification factor, the guide number can be adapted with the following formula:

$$L2 = L1 + 5V$$

where L1 = normal guide number, L2 = required guide number, and V = deviation factor.

Index